AF166673

Foreword

RE and Literacy in the Classroom is a three-book series written to help schools meet the requirements of Religious Education in the classroom. It sits easily beside the non-statutory national expectations and the QCA scheme of work.

RE teaching is most effective when it includes both learning about religion (AT1) and learning from religion (AT2). Therefore, each eight-page unit of work includes one activity from each attainment target, covering:

- knowledge and understanding of religious beliefs and teachings; religious practices and lifestyles; and ways of expressing meaning;

- the skill of asking and responding to questions of identity and experience; meaning and purpose; and values and commitments.

This will help children to learn about Christianity and the other principal religions, as well as develop their ability to think about and respond to what they have learnt.

Each book contains a selection of the world's greatest sacred stories from different faiths. Each unit is based upon one of these sacred stories, retold through text and pictures. The accompanying activities include an exploration of the different faiths and their beliefs with an underpinning of good literacy practice. This brings language and communication into partnership with RE. The literacy opportunities in each unit include:

- a sacred story for discussion and study;

- presentation of their own ideas using different writing genres; and

- a relevant word or text activity from the Literacy Strategy scheme of work.

The accompanying comprehensive teachers notes provide curriculum links, story references, discussion points, resource lists and answers.

The three books in this series are:

RE and Literacy in the Classroom Book 1 (Ages 5–7)

RE and Literacy in the Classroom Book 2 (Ages 7–9)

RE and Literacy in the Classroom Book 3 (Ages 9–11).

Contents

Teachers Notes

Each eight-page unit of work starts with three pages of comprehensive teachers notes. The information provided in these teachers notes includes:

The religion from which the sacred story is derived.

Table of curriculum links to show how the activities fit into the following curricular requirements for Year 5 and 6 pupils:

- RE Non-statutory Guidance
- RE QCA Scheme of Work
- National Literacy Strategy

The third (RE AT1), fouth (RE AT2) and fifth (Literacy Strategy) copymasters are also explained in further detail. The teachers notes on these activities may include some of the following:

- preparation
- introduction
- discussion
- additional/extension activities
- resources
- answers.

David the Shepherd Boy

Teachers Notes

Religion: Judaism

Curriculum Links:

R.E. Attainment Target 1: Learning about Religions
- Beliefs and teachings – describe religious beliefs and teachings and their importance.

R.E. Attainment Target 2: Learning from Religion
- Meanings and purpose – ask questions about the significant experiences of key figures from religions studied.

QCA R.E. Scheme of Work Reference
- 5C – Where did the Christian Bible come from?

National Literacy Strategy Reference
- Year 5, Term 3, Text 1 – investigate texts from different cultures.

Story Reference:
The Bible 1 Samuel, Chapters 16 – 18.
A Tapestry of Tales by Sandra Palmer and Elizabeth Breuilly (Collins Educational, 1993).
Stories from the Jewish World (MacDonald, 1988).
Storyteller Series: Jewish Stories by Anita Ganeri (Evans Brothers, 2001).
Modern World Religions: Judaism (Heinemann Educational Publishers, 2002).

Notes – Pages 29 and 30 – David the Shepherd Boy:

Introduction/Discussion:
- Discuss the wealth of detail in the Bible story, which shows us how unlikely it was that a young boy like David could defeat the giant.
- What does the Bible suggest was the reason for David's success?
- Discuss the extraordinary changes in David's life and expectations – from working as a shepherd boy for his father to becoming the King of Israel.
- Explain that the battle between David and Goliath is one of the most famous stories in the Old Testament. David is still a popular name around the world. There are many works of art showing David as a young hero, including the famous statue by Michelangelo.
- Discuss why a story about a small but brave person defeating a giant has remained so popular.

RE and Literacy in the Classroom • 26 • Prim-Ed Publishing –www .prim-ed.com

The story reference has been included for teachers wishing to do further work on the sacred story.

Introductory activities and discussion points based on the sacred story.

The first two copymaster pages in each unit are a sacred story from one of the major faiths. The stories are retold through text and pictures. Teachers can use the stories in a variety of ways to suit their own routines and the age and ability of their class. The story may be read aloud to the class or group by the teacher or may be distributed to children to read individually, in pairs or in small groups. Children will often benefit from having their own copy of the text to refer to when completing the subsequent activities. Alternatively, teachers could display the story page on an overhead projector for the class, use a single enlarged photocopy for group reading, or make a few photocopies and laminate them as a permanent resource for the class. The stories could also be used as the basis for an assembly.

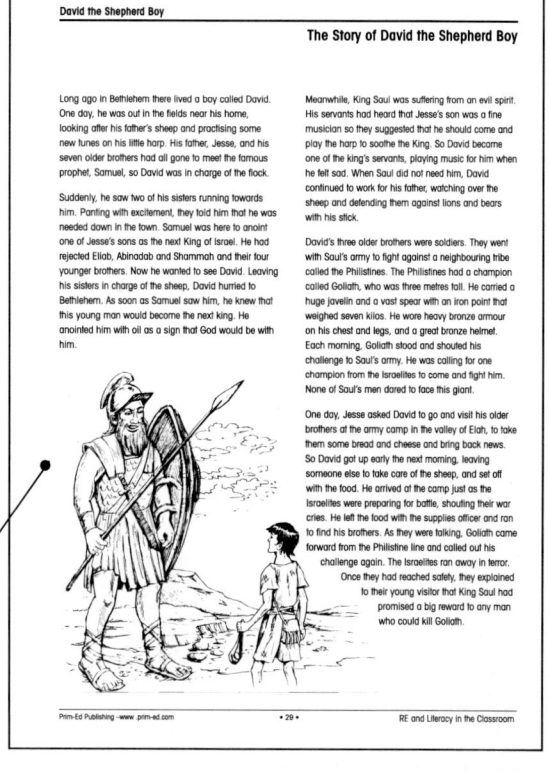

David the Shepherd Boy

The Story of David the Shepherd Boy

Long ago in Bethlehem there lived a boy called David. One day, he was out in the fields near his home, looking after his father's sheep and practising some new tunes on his little harp. His father, Jesse, and his seven older brothers had all gone to meet the famous prophet, Samuel, so David was in charge of the flock.

Suddenly, he saw two of his sisters running towards him. Panting with excitement, they told him that he was needed down in the town. Samuel was here to anoint one of Jesse's sons as the next King of Israel. He had rejected Eliab, Abinadab and Shammah and their four younger brothers. Now he wanted to see David. Leaving his sisters in charge of the sheep, David hurried to Bethlehem. As soon as Samuel saw him, he knew that this young man would become the next king. He anointed him with oil as a sign that God would be with him.

Meanwhile, King Saul was suffering from an evil spirit. His servants had heard that Jesse's son was a fine musician so they suggested that he should come and play the harp to soothe the King. So David became one of the king's servants, playing music for him when he felt sad. When Saul did not need him, David continued to work for his father, watching over the sheep and defending them against lions and bears with his stick.

David's three older brothers were soldiers. They went with Saul's army to fight against a neighbouring tribe called the Philistines. The Philistines had a champion called Goliath, who was three metres tall. He carried a huge javelin and a vast spear with an iron point that weighed seven kilos. He wore heavy bronze armour on his chest and legs, and a great bronze helmet. Each morning, Goliath stood and shouted his challenge to Saul's army. He was calling for one champion for the Israelites to come and fight him. None of Saul's men dared to face this giant.

One day, Jesse asked David to go and visit his older brothers at the army camp in the valley of Elah, to take them some bread and cheese and bring back news. So David got up early the next morning, leaving someone else to take care of the sheep, and set off with the food. He arrived at the camp just as the Israelites were preparing for battle, shouting their war cries. He left the food with the supplies officer and ran to find his brothers. As they were talking, Goliath came forward from the Philistine lines and called out his challenge again. The Israelites ran away in terror. Once they had reached safety, they explained to their young visitor that King Saul had promised a big reward to any man who could kill Goliath.

Prim-Ed Publishing –www .prim-ed.com • 29 • RE and Literacy in the Classroom

Religious Education and Literacy in the Classroom

Book 3

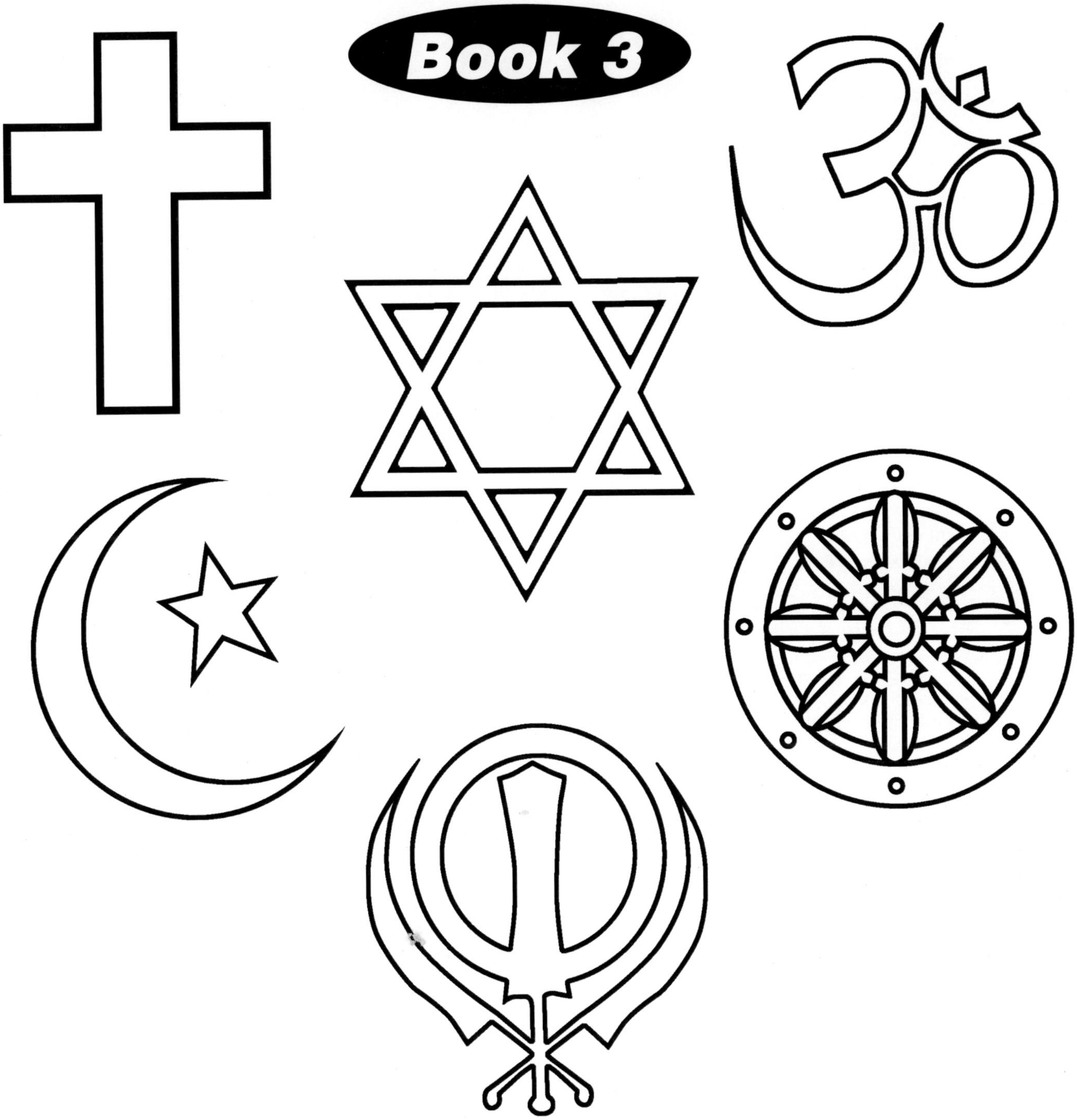

E. Freedman and J. Keys

Prim-Ed
Publishing
www.prim-ed.com

**Religious Education and Literacy
in the Classroom—Book 3**
Prim-Ed Publishing

Published in 2004 by Prim-Ed Publishing

Copyright E. Freedman and J. Keys 2004

ISBN 1 86400 789 3
PR–2323

Additional titles available in this series are:
Religious Education and Literacy in the Classroom—Book 1
Religious Education and Literacy in the Classroom—Book 2

Home Page: http://www.prim-ed.com

Prim-Ed Publishing Pty Ltd
Offices in: Bosheen, New Ross, Co. Wexford, Ireland   Email: sales@prim-ed.com

Internet websites
In some cases, websites or specific URLs may be recommended. While these are checked and rechecked at the time of publication, the
publisher has no control over any subsequent changes which may be made to webpages. It is *strongly* recommended that the class teacher
checks *all* URLs before allowing students to access them.

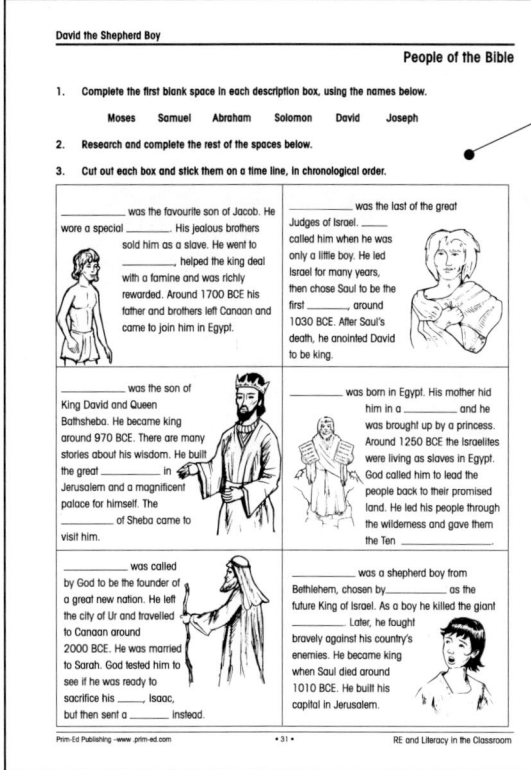

The third copymaster in each unit is an activity based on the AT1 non-statutory guidelines in RE. Children will be asked to recount or retell the stories. This covers learning about religions, showing knowledge and understanding of what people believe, what they do and how they express their beliefs. This page may be used as either part of a specific RE lesson or as a text-level activity during the Literacy Hour.

The fourth copymaster in each unit is intended to stimulate discussion based around the requirements of the AT2 non-statutory guidelines in RE. Children are encouraged to respond to stories from different religions by relating them to their own life and experience. They will compare aspects of their own experience with those of others.

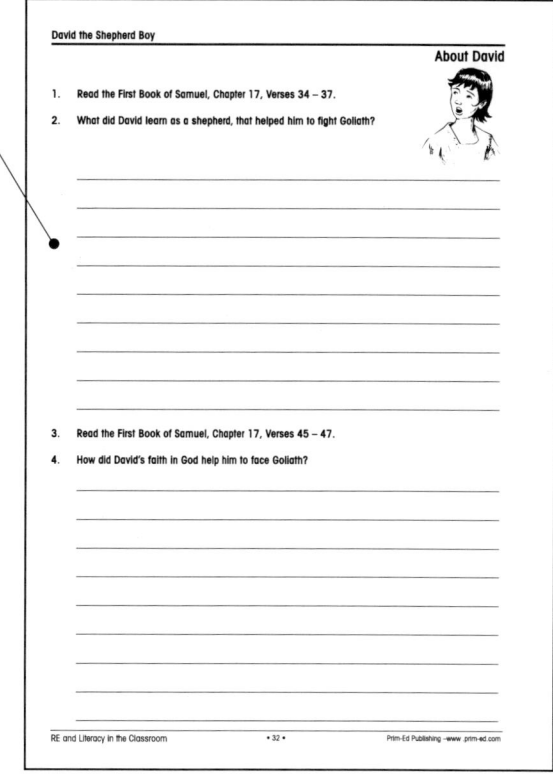

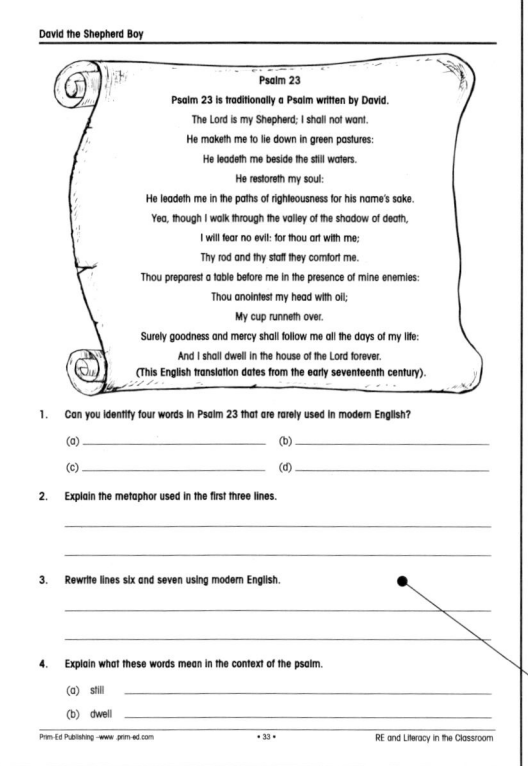

The fifth and final copymaster in each unit offers a variety of Literacy Strategy independent word and text-level work, all based on the sacred story.

Page iv contains religion–based merit certificates. These can be photocopied onto coloured paper or card and given to children to encourage them to try their best and promote their self-esteem. These certificates will also help to provide a positive working environment.

Pages v–xi include graphics from the major faiths covered in this series, to be used as clip art, to complement your teaching programme. They have a multitude of uses including display and pupil and teacher reference.

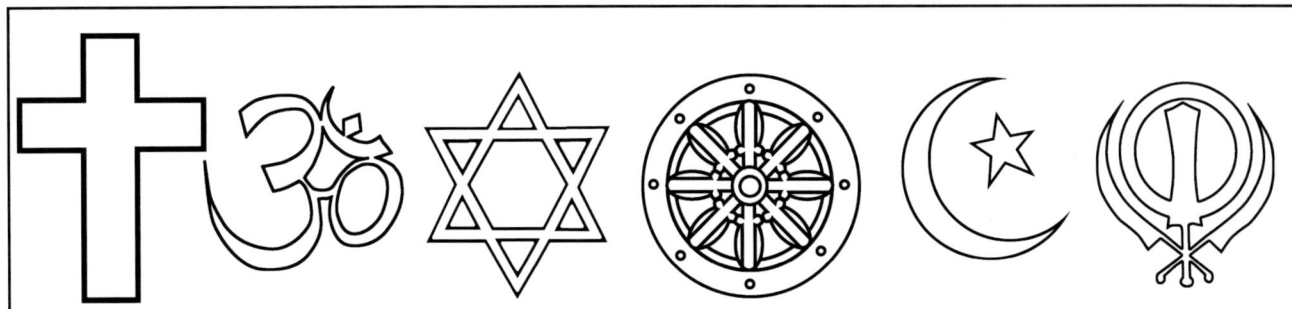

Great R. E. Work!

Name: _____

Date: _____ Signed: _____

Super Effort!

Name: _____

Awarded for:

Signed: _____

Date: _____

Star R.E. Pupil

Name: _____

Signed: _____

Date: _____

Judaism Clip Art

Sikhism Clip Art

Teachers Notes

Religion: Christianity

Curriculum Links:

R.E. Attainment Target 1: Learning about Religions • Beliefs and teachings – describe religious beliefs and teachings and their importance. • Expression and language – make links between religious symbols, language and stories and the beliefs or ideas that underline them.
R.E. Attainment Target 2: Learning from Religion • Identity and experience – compare aspects of their own experiences and those of others, identifying what influences their lives. • Values and commitments – make links between values, including religious ones and their own attitudes or behaviours.
QCA R.E. Scheme of Work Reference • 5C – Where did the Christian Bible come from? • 6C – Why are sacred texts important?
National Literacy Strategy Reference • Year 5, Term 2, Text 11 – write own versions. • Year 5, Term 2, Text 12 – use the structures of poems to write extensions.

Story Reference:

Various Bibles, including *The New English Bible, The Good News Bible* and *The New International Bible.*
Discovering Sacred Texts: The Bible (Heinemann, 1994).
World Beliefs and Cultures: Christianity by Sue Penny (Heinemann, 2000).
World Religions: Christianity by Katherine Prior (Franklin Watts, 1999).
Christians by John Drone (Lion, 1994).

Notes – Page 6 – In the Beginning:

Introduction:

- The Bible, which was written by many different people over more than 1000 years, is a special book for Christians. It is made up of 66 books and is sometimes considered a 'library' rather than a book.
- Christians think of the Bible in two parts: the Old Testament and the New Testament. The Old Testament (39 books) contains the Scriptures (sacred writings), history, poetry and prophesy of the Jewish people. The New Testament (27 books) is made up of writings about Jesus and his first followers. Together these books are an inspiration and guide to Christians in their daily life.
- The first five books of the Old Testament are sometimes known as the Torah (a word which means 'teaching'); these are the sacred scriptures of the Jewish people. The words of the Old Testament were passed on in an oral tradition until eventually written down in Hebrew.
- The New Testament is a collection of the accounts of Jesus' life, the gospels, written in Greek about 150 years after Jesus' death. Letters of advice written by the apostles to the early Christians (the epistles) are also part of the New Testament.
- Early Bibles were very precious. They were generally highly illustrated and due to their rarity were often chained up to prevent them from being stolen.

Discussion:

- Why are there different versions of the same events in the Bible?
- Why did it take so long for both the Old Testament and the New Testament to be written down?
- When the Bible was translated from Latin into other languages, why did it take so long?
- Why does the Christian Bible include the Torah and other Jewish writing?
- What did Jesus read and study when he was a boy?
- Why has the Bible influenced Western art and literature?

Extension:

- Choose a Bible story. Give the children a number of Bibles, including a Children's Bible. Ask the children to make a list of the differences they find, particularly between the Children's Bible and the other Bibles.
- Investigate people who have been closely associated with the Bible, such as William Tyndale, who translated the New Testament into English in the 16th Century.

Resources:

- Pencil or pen and paper
- Different Bibles, including a children's Bible

Notes – Page 7 – The Old Testament and New Testament:

Introduction/Discussion:

- To show the scale of the Bible, stack 66 books, one on top of the other. Stack the 39 Old Testament books first and then the 27 New Testament books. Then join the two stacks together.
- Explain the categories of the books to the children – 5 Teaching, 17 History, 5 Poetry, 18 Prophesy and 21 Letters.
- Discuss what each of the categories means. Have a biblical example from each set of books for children to read and discuss. In groups, research a set of books and write a description for the rest of the class.
- Good examples are:

Old Testament, Teaching:
- Genesis, Chapter 2 – The Garden of Eden
- Exodus, Chapter 14 – Crossing the Red Sea

Old Testament, History:
- 1 Samuel, Chapter 16 – David is King
- 2 Chronicles, Chapter 9 – Queen of Sheba

Old Testament, Poetry:
- Psalm 23 – The Lord is my Shepherd
- Proverbs, Chapter 12, Verse 23

Old Testament, Prophesy:
- Isaiah, Chapter 13 – Punishing Babylon
- Malachi, Chapter 4 – Day of the Lord is Coming

New Testament, History:
- Matthew, Chapter 18 – Lost Sheep Parable
- Acts, Chapter 9 – Conversion of Saul

New Testament, Letters (Epistles):
- Romans, Chapter 1 – Paul's Letter to the Romans
- 1 John, Chapter 3 – Love One Another

New Testament, Prophesy:
- Revelations, Chapter 7 – The Enormous Crowd

Resources:

- Pencil or pen
- 66 books
- Bibles
- Non-fiction Christianity books
- ICT opportunity – use a computer with the Internet or CD–ROM encyclopaedia for research

Answers:

1. **Teaching:** Genesis; Exodus; Leviticus; Numbers; Deuteronomy.
   History: Joshua; Judges; Ruth; 1 Samuel; 2 Samuel; 1 Kings; 2 Kings; 1 Chronicles; 2 Chronicles; Ezra; Nehemiah; Esther.
   Poetry: Job; Psalms; Proverbs; Ecclesiastes; Song of Solomon.
   Prophesy: Isaiah; Jeremiah; Lamentations; Ezekiel; Daniel; Hosea; Joel; Amos; Obadiah; Jonah; Micah; Nahum; Habakkuk; Zephaniah; Haggai; Zechariah; Malachi.
2. **History:** Matthew; Mark; Luke; John; Acts.
   Letters: Romans; 1 Corinthians; 2 Corinthians; Galations; Ephesians; Philippians; Colossians; 1 Thessalonians; 2 Thessalonians; 1 Timothy; 2 Timothy; Titus; Philemon; Hebrews; James; 1 Peter; 2 Peter; 1 John; 2 John; 3 John; Jude.
   Prophesy: Revelation.

Notes – Page 8 – The Bible Today:

Extension:

- Choose one of the Bible references, either from the sheet or one of own choice. Create an item for display depicting the biblical message and how it might help today. Display work.
- Find references to the Bible in the world around them. They could be in advertising, in proverbs, in language etc. (The word 'Judas' is a good example.)

Resources:

- Pencil or pen and crayons
- Bibles
- ICT opportunity – computer with word processing and art programs

Answers:

2. Teacher check – accept any answer which shows pupils have read the text and thought about it. Possible answers are listed below, but pupils may deduce different messages. This is an opportunity to discuss their thinking and reasoning.
   (a) It is important to accept what happens in our lives and to forgive those we think have wronged us. We do not always understand God's will, which may not become apparent for many years, and sometimes never will.
   (b) Wisdom is very important in helping us make decisions in our life. Wisdom is knowing the best way to deal with all parts of our life. We should look to others to provide wisdom and also pass our wisdom on to others.
   Note: When Solomon was asked what he wanted by God, he asked for wisdom. The Book of Proverbs is full of wisdom and advice. Pupils could be given the opportunity to look from Chapter 8 to the end of Proverbs to find advice (Proverbs) which they like and might suggest to others.
   (c) Don't let material things get in the way of loving God, following his laws and helping one another. Don't let 'the law' become more important than your common sense and the laws of God. These are all lessons for life.
   (d) Listen for the Word of God. Be open to his message and do not persecute those you do not understand.

Notes – Page 9 – Creation Psalm:

Introduction:

- A psalm is a song, poem or prayer that praises God.
- There are 150 sacred psalms in the Book of Psalms (Old Testament).

Extension:

- Compare this psalm with *The Canticle of Creatures* by St Francis of Assisi, which also celebrates what God has done.
- The psalm could be compared to other poems or songs written about the prophets and leaders in other religions and the great things they have done.
- Write own poem describing the creation by God, using the ideas from Genesis and Psalm 8.

Resources:

- Pencil or pen and crayons
- Bibles
- *The Canticle of Creatures* by St Francis of Assisi (see page 22).

Answers:

2. Teacher check, but possible answers include:

Words used in the psalm we no longer use today	Meaning of the word
Thy	Your
Thine	Your
Thou	You
Sucklings	Babies
Hast	Has
Madest	Made
Yea	Yes
Passeth	Passed

In the beginning, when God created the universe, the earth was formless and desolate. The raging ocean that covered everything was engulfed in total darkness, and the Spirit of God was moving over the water.

Then God commanded, 'Let there be light' – and light appeared. God was pleased with what he saw. Then he separated the light from the darkness, and he named the light 'day' and the darkness 'night'. Evening passed and morning came – that was the first day.

Then God commanded, 'Let there be a dome to divide the water and to keep it in two separate places' – and it was done. So God made a dome, and it separated the water under it from the water above it. He named the dome 'sky'. Evening passed and morning came – that was the second day.

Then God commanded, 'Let the water below the sky come together in one place, so that the land will appear' – and it was done. He named the land 'earth', and the water which had come together he named 'sea'. And God was pleased with what he saw. Then he commanded, 'Let the earth produce all kinds of plants, those that bear grain and those that bear fruit' – and it was done. So the earth produced all kinds of plants, and God was pleased with what he saw. Evening passed and morning came – that was the third day.

Then God commanded, 'Let light appear in the sky to separate day from night and to show the time when days, years, and religious festivals begin; they will shine in the sky to give light to the earth' – and it was done. So God made the two larger lights, the sun to rule over the day and the moon to rule over the night; he also made the stars. He placed the lights in the sky to shine on the earth, to rule over the day and the night, and to separate light from darkness. And God was pleased with what he saw. Evening passed and morning came – that was the fourth day.

Then God commanded, 'Let the water be filled with many kinds of living beings, and let the air be filled with birds.' So God created the great sea monsters, all kinds of creatures that live in the water, and all kinds of birds. And God was pleased with what he saw. He blessed them all and told the creatures that live in the water to reproduce and to fill the sea, and he told the birds to increase in number. Evening passed and morning came – that was the fifth day.

Then God commanded, 'Let the earth produce all kinds of animal life: domestic and wild, large and small' – and it was done. So God made them all, and he was pleased with what he saw.

Then God said, 'And now we will make human beings; they will be like us and resemble us. They will have power over the fish, the birds, and all animals, domestic and wild, large and small'. So God created human beings, making them to be like himself. He created them male and female, blessed them, and said, 'Have many children, so that your descendants will live all over the earth and bring it under their control. I am putting you in charge of the fish, the birds, and all wild animals. I have provided all kinds of grain and all kinds of fruit for you to eat; but for all the wild animals and for all the birds I have provided grass and leafy plants for food' – and it was done. God looked at everything he had made, and he was very pleased. Evening passed and morning came – that was the sixth day.

And so the whole universe was completed. By the seventh day God finished what he had been doing and stopped working. He blessed the seventh day and set it apart as a special day, because by that day he had completed his creation and stopped working. And that is how the universe was created.

© The Good News Bible.

The Old Testament and New Testament

The Christian holy book is called the Bible. It is a collection of books made up of two main sections, which Christians call the Old Testament and the New Testament. Testament means 'agreement'.

1. **Write the names on the Old Testament books.**

2. **Write the names on the New Testament books.**

The Bible Today

The Bible is used today by many people, to help them in their daily lives.
They find inspiration, they learn how to behave and they learn how to accept
the trials of life.

1.   **Read the following passages from the Bible.**

2.   **Write the main message and how this might help someone in their life.**

(a)
Genesis, Chapters 45 – 46

The main message is _____

_____

It might help by _____

_____

(b)
Proverbs, Chapter 8

The main message is _____

_____

It might help by _____

_____

(c)
Mark, Chapter 12

The main message is _____

_____

It might help by _____

_____

(d)
Acts, Chapter 9

The main message is _____

_____

It might help by _____

_____

Creation Psalm

The Psalms of King David are songs and poems that praise God. They were written a long time ago. Psalm 8 is about the creation of the world, written in Genesis.

1. Read Psalm 8.

Psalm 8

O Lord our Lord, how excellent is thy name in all the earth!
Who hast set thy glory above the heavens,
Out of the mouth of babes and sucklings hast thou ordained
strength because of thine enemies,
That thou mightest still the enemy and the avenger.
When I consider thy heavens,
The work of thy fingers,
The moon and the stars,
Which thou hast ordained;
What is man, that thou art mindful of him?
And the son of man, that thou visitest him?
For thou hast made him a little lower than the angels,
And hast crowned him with glory and honour.
Thou madest him to have dominion over the works of thy hands;
Thou hast put all things under his feet,
All sheep and oxen,
Yea, and the beasts of the field;
The fowl of the air, and the fish of the sea,
And whatsoever passeth through the paths of the seas.
O Lord our Lord, how excellent is thy name in all the earth!

2. Complete the table.

Words used in the psalm we no longer use today	Meaning of the word

Religion: Christianity

Curriculum Links:

R.E. Attainment Target 1: Learning about Religions
- Beliefs and teachings – describe religious beliefs and teachings and their importance.

R.E. Attainment Target 2: Learning from Religion
- Identity and experience – compare aspects of their own experiences and those of others, identifying what influences their lives.
- Meaning and purpose – compare their own and other people's ideas about questions that are difficult to answer.

QCA R.E. Scheme of Work Reference
- 5D – How do the beliefs of Christians influence their actions?

National Literacy Strategy Reference
- Year 5, Term 3, Text 7 – write from another character's point of view.

Story Reference:
The Bible: Luke, Chapter 10, Verses 30 – 37.
World Beliefs and Cultures: Christianity by Sue Penny (Heinemann, 2000).
World Religions: Christianity by Katherine Prior (Franklin Watts, 1999).
Christians by John Drone (Lion, 1994).
What do we Know about Christianity? (Macdonald Young Books, 1995).
Discovering Sacred Texts: The Bible (Heinemann, 1994).

Notes – Pages 12 and 13 – The Good Samaritan:

Introduction/Discussion:
- Discuss the meaning of the word 'parable'.
- When introducing this parable, it is important to read the verses preceding the parable itself (verses 25 – 29), as these set the scene. The parable is addressing 'Who is my neighbour?' It is poignant as the Jews and the Samaritans were enemies at this time. Therefore, Jesus is trying to say 'Even your enemy is your neighbour'.
- After the children have read the parable, ask them to think of parallels in the modern world.
- The discussion could focus on 'out of school' issues; e.g. homelessness, asylum seekers etc. Or the focus could be on 'in school' issues; e.g. bullying, travellers or newcomers.

Extension:
- Write a modern parable, based on one of the issues discussed above. What 'message' is the parable trying to convey?

Resources:
- Pencil or pen and paper
- Different Bibles, including a children's Bible

Notes – Page 14 – The Good Samaritan:

Introduction:

- Recap the story before the children begin this activity.

Resources:

- Pencil or pen and crayons
- A copy of *The Good Samaritan* story

Answers:

1. (a) no (b) no (c) yes (d) no
2. Teacher check – encourage children to be empathetic in their thinking.

Notes – Page 15 – What Should I Do?:

Introduction/Discussion:

- Recap the 'in school' and 'out of school' issues which were raised after the initial reading of *The Good Samaritan*.
- Children should work in pairs or small groups to brainstorm the situations before beginning to write their views.

Resources:

- Pencil or pen and crayons

Answers:

Teacher check – encourage children to be empathetic in their thinking.

Notes – Pages 16 and 17 – My Story:

Introduction/Discussion:

- Children need to understand that in biblical times a traveller would have been at risk on the lonely road from Jerusalem to Jericho. It may be that the priest and the Levite were afraid that the thieves who had attacked and robbed the traveller might return. Also, at that time, the Samaritans and the Jews were enemies. Therefore, the traveller who was a Jew might have been very surprised that the Samaritan stopped to help him. This may have been why Jesus used a Samaritan in the parable.
- Encourage the children to think about the story from more than one point of view, before choosing one point of view for their version. Discuss why they chose that particular point of view.

Extension:

- The 'rewritten' parables could be taped and played back to the class.

Resources:

- Pencil or pen
- ICT opportunity – tape recorder

Answers:

Teacher check

The Good Samaritan

A man was travelling from Jerusalem to Jericho.

The man was set upon by thieves. They stole his goods and his clothes. They beat and kicked him.

The thieves left the man for dead by the roadside.

A priest passed by. He saw the man, but continued walking.

Then a Levite walked by. He had a quick look at the man, but walked by on the opposite side of the road.

The Good Samaritan

The next person to come along the road was a Samaritan. He saw the man and was filled with pity.

The Samaritan cleaned the wounds and bandaged them.

The Samaritan helped the man onto his own donkey.

The Samaritan took the man to the nearest inn. There he took a room and food for the man.

When the Samaritan left the next day, he left money with the innkeeper, so the man could have whatever he needed.

The Good Samaritan

Jesus told the Parable of The Good Samaritan to illustrate the law.

1. **Which law do you think Jesus was trying to illustrate? Colour yes or no.**

    (a) Love your God with all your heart, soul and mind. | yes | no |

    (b) Obey the Commandments of God. | yes | no |

    (c) Love thy neighbour as thyself. | yes | no |

    (d) Live a life of love and joy. | yes | no |

2. **Answer the following questions in sentences.**

    (a) What did the priest and the Levite think when they saw the man? _____

    _____

    _____

    (b) Why didn't they stop to help the man? _____

    _____

    _____

    (c) What did the Samaritan think when he saw the man?

    _____

    _____

    _____

    (d) The Samaritan didn't know the man, so why did he stop to help? _____

    _____

    _____

    _____

    _____

    (e) What message is Jesus giving through this story? _____

    _____

    _____

    _____

What Should I Do?

1. **Look at these situations. Write what the priest or Levite and the Good Samaritan would have done in each situation.**

(a)

The priest or Levite would _____

_____

_____

The Good Samaritan would _____

_____

_____

(b)

The priest or Levite would _____

_____

_____

The Good Samaritan would _____

_____

_____

(c)

The priest or Levite would _____

_____

_____

The Good Samaritan would _____

_____

_____

2. **Draw a different imaginary situation. Write what the priest or Levite and the Good Samaritan would have done in the situation.**

The situation: _____

_____

_____

The priest or Levite would _____

_____

_____

_____

The Good Samaritan would _____

_____

_____

_____

In the Parable of The Good Samaritan, Jesus told his disciples that we should behave as the Good Samaritan did. Is there another point of view for this story?

1.　(a)　**Write notes on the important facts of the story, from the point of view of each of these people.**

　　(b)　**Write reasons why each person acted as he or she did.**

The Priest

Important fact: _____

_____

_____

_____

Why I acted as I did: _____

_____

_____

_____

Important fact: _____

_____

_____

_____

Why I acted as I did: _____

_____

_____

_____

The Levite

The Traveller

Important fact: _____

_____

_____

_____

Why I acted as I did: _____

_____

_____

_____

2. Choose one of the people on page 16. Rewrite the story of *The Good Samaritan* from his point of view.

Religion: Christianity

Curriculum Links:

R.E. Attainment Target 1: Learning about Religions
- Beliefs and teachings – describe religious beliefs and teachings and their importance.
- Practices and lifestyles – show understanding of the ways of belonging to a religion and what these involve.

R.E. Attainment Target 2: Learning from Religion
- Values and commitments – ask questions about matters of right and wrong and show understanding of moral and religious issues.

QCA R.E. Scheme of Work Reference
- 6A – Worship and community.

National Literacy Strategy Reference
- Year 6, Term 2, Text 18 – construct effective arguments.

Story Reference:

The Life of St Francis by Rachel Billington (Hodder, 1999).
Religious Education Topics (Longman, 1989).
Christians by John Drone (Lion, 1994).

Notes – Pages 21 and 22 – St Francis of Assisi/The Canticle of Creatures:

Introduction:
- What is a religious community? Have the children heard of anyone who has started a religious community? (Answers might include Mother Theresa or Gandhi.)
- Do the children know of any organisations – religious and non-religious – which work to help others? Children could look at recent local newspapers, which often report on events run by these organisations.

Discussion:
- What sort of man was Francis?
- What did Francis believe? What did he do to live his beliefs?
- How does the life Francis chose reflect the life Jesus said his followers should live?
- Can the children think of any other people who have dedicated their life to good work, as Francis chose to do?
- Can the children think of little ways in which they can follow some of the ways of Francis?
- Does the life of Francis have modern parallels? Is there anyone in the modern world that Francis reminds the children of? How do people today display similar dedication?

Extension:

- Research another religious community: a Christian community from the Middle Ages (the same time as the Franciscans) or one from a different religion. (Buddhists have many of the same ideals as Francis in relation to living things.)
- Research another non-religious community that works in the world today, helping others; e.g. Médecins sans Frontières.
- Look at the series of frescoes painted by Giotto between 1295 and 1300. They depict the life of St Francis. These can be found on the 'Web Gallery of Art' on the Internet (www.kfki.hu/~arthp/tours/giotto/francis.html). As well as a gallery tour of the frescoes, there is information on Francis and his life and about the painter Giotto and the frescoes he painted to honour Francis.
- In groups, children could look at one part of the Canticle; e.g. 'our Brother the Sun' or 'our Sister the moon'. They could write a new description and make a class canticle of creatures.
- Produce a timeline, illustrating the important points in Francis' life.

Resources:

- Pencil, pen, paper and crayons
- Local newspapers
- ICT opportunity – use a computer with the Internet or CD-ROM encyclopaedia for research

Notes – Page 23 – Christian Worship and Community:

Introduction/Discussion:

- Discuss different forms of worship.
- Discuss whether worship has to be carried out within a church. (Look particularly at non-Christian worship.)
- Where else can people worship?
- Where did Francis worship? (Outdoors, but also in a church.)
- Compare different forms of Christian worship. Perhaps invite members of different Christian faiths to come in and talk to the children about their worship.

Resources:

- Pencil or pen
- Non-fiction Christianity books for research
- ICT opportunity – use a computer with the Internet or CD-ROM encyclopaedia for research

Answers:

1(a) Most Christians worship in churches. However, churches can be very different and churches in one part of the world can be very different to those in another part of the world. If there is a large gathering, worship might take place outdoors, e.g. when the Pope visits.

1(b) Christians worship when they gather together, including in someone's home. They worship during festivals (e.g. Easter) and services (e.g. Christmas carol services).

1(c) The main difference is in the simplicity of the Friends' Meeting house.

2 – 3. Teacher check

Notes – Page 24 – Christian Communities:

Additional Information:

- Children will need access to relevant information for the completion of this activity. Non-fiction books, CD-ROM encyclopaedias and the Internet all contain information.
- Web addresses for the Christian communities covered on the copymaster are:
    The Salvation Army: www1.salvationarmy.org
    Christian Aid: www.christian-aid.org
    Oxfam: www.oxfam.org
    The Friars Minor (Franciscans): www.ofm.org
- Visits by representatives of the communities listed and other Christian communities will help children to more fully understand their work.

Extension:

- The research into the various communities could include an investigation of how these charities are funded and how they spend their budgets. (This information is usually available from the charities themselves.)

Resources:

- Pencil or pen
- Members of the Christian communities
- Non-fiction books on Christian communities for research
- ICT opportunity – use a computer with the Internet or CD-ROM encyclopaedia for research

Answers:

Teacher check.

Notes – Page 25 – I Think ... :

Introduction/Discussion:

- In groups, discuss and marshal thoughts about the arguments raised on the copymaster.

Extension:

- Children could survey the wider community's thoughts on these issues.
- A display of arguments could help children to think about their contribution.

Resources:

- Pencil or pen
- ICT opportunity – use a computer with the Internet for research

Answers:

Teacher check

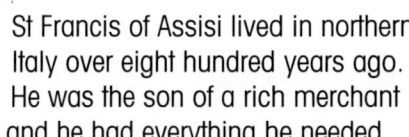

St Francis of Assisi lived in northern Italy over eight hundred years ago. He was the son of a rich merchant and he had everything he needed.

When he was a young man, a war broke out and he went away to fight. He was captured and thrown into prison. While in prison he began to think about God, and how he could do more to praise and worship God. When he returned from the war, God spoke to him and asked for his help. At first he thought he could use his father's wealth to do as God asked, but then realised that this would not do.

Francis decided to give up everything he had and to follow God, to help others. He worshipped God in church wherever he went, but he also worshipped God in everything he did. He wore rough clothes, he walked barefoot and he ate only enough to live on. He worked with the beggars and the lepers; he showed everyone his love of God.

Francis believed that we should not only 'Love our neighbours', but that we should love all living things. He believed that this is how we should show our love for God. Francis loved animals, and he believed that in talking to animals he was talking to God. One day he saw a flock of birds waiting to eat the seed the farmer was sowing. He said to the birds 'Dear birds, God has given you everything you need. You must praise him and leave the farmer's seed to grow'. The birds followed Francis from the field.

On another occasion he came to a town which was terrorised by a wolf. Francis went to talk to the wolf. He said, 'Dear wolf, you are hungry, come with me'. The wolf followed Francis. Francis told the townspeople that the wolf was hungry. So the townspeople fed the wolf and he did not attack them or their animals.

At this time the Christian church had become very rich and powerful. Bishops, priests and monks lived in luxury. Francis believed that Christians should live a simpler life and that the priests and monks should live like their flocks. He said that Jesus was a poor man in the service of poor people and that his church should be the same.

Francis started a new religious community called the Friars Minor, also known as the Franciscans. These monks would be teachers and tenders of the sick, they would be missionaries and stay in their own communities, but always they would devote themselves to a life of prayer and helping the poor. They would own nothing, but would worship God with their people.

Francis worshipped God in all things, and he talked to God through his songs and poems. Many people learned about God from Francis.

The Canticle of Creatures

Praised be my Lord God
with all his creatures, and especially our
Brother the Sun, who brings us the day and
who brings us the light; fair is he and shines
with a very great splendour.
Praised be my Lord for our Sister the
Moon, and for the stars, which he
has set clear and lovely in heaven.
Praised be my Lord for our brother
the Wind, and for air and cloud,
calms and all weather, by which
thou upholdest life in all creatures.
Praised be my Lord for our Sister
Water, who is very serviceable unto us and
humble and precious and clean.
Praised be my Lord for our Brother Fire, through whom thou givest us
light in the darkness; and he is bright and pleasant and very mighty and strong.
Praised be my Lord for our Mother the Earth, which doth sustain us and keep us,
and bringeth forth divers fruits, and flowers of many colours, and grass.
Praised be my Lord for all those who pardon one another for his love's sake,
and who endure weakness and tribulation; blessed are they who
peacably shall endure, for thou, O most highest, shall give them
a crown.
Praised be my Lord for our Sister Death of the body,
from which no man escapeth ...
Praise ye and bless the Lord, and give
thanks unto him, and serve him with
great humility.

 Prim-Ed Publishing – www.prim-ed.com

Christian Worship and Community

Francis worshipped God in everything he did. He gave his life to worshipping God.

1. (a) How do most Christians worship God? _____

   _____

   (b) Can you think of other ways that Christians worship? _____

   _____

   (c) Research the main difference between worship in a church and a Friends' Meeting.

Church	Friends' Meeting

Francis talked to God through his songs and poems. Christians talk to God through prayers, hymns and poetry.

2. (a) List the names of some prayers. _____

   _____

   (b) Which prayer do you like the best? _____

   Why? _____

   (c) Explain the meaning of your chosen prayer. _____

   _____

Francis believed that all living things should be important to Christian communities.

3. (a) Do you agree? | yes | no |

   (b) How can Christians take care of the poor living in their community? _____

   _____

   _____

   (c) How can Christians look after other living things?_____

   _____

   _____

   _____

   _____

   _____

Christian Communities

Christian communities try to support all members of the community. Many Christian communities also try to help people in other countries, or others in society who need help.

Research the following Christian communities. Draw their logos and answer the questions.

Community logo	Who are the members?	Who do they help?	How do they help?
The Salvation Army			
Christian Aid			
Oxfam			
The Friars Minor (Franciscans)			

I Think...

I think Christian communities should do more to help the homeless.

I think Christian communities should do more for their own community.

I think Christian communities should do more to help the people in poor countries.

1. **Choose one of the above statements. Think about how the issue makes you feel.**

2. **Research and list the points that you will use to write your argument.**

   (a) Argument chosen: _____

   _____

   (b) Important points:

   • _____

   • _____

   • _____

   • _____

   • _____

   (c) Supporting points:

   • _____

   • _____

   • _____

   • _____

   • _____

   (d) Possible objections:

   • _____

   • _____

   • _____

   • _____

   • _____

3. **Write or word process your argument. Try your argument on a friend.**

Teachers Notes

Religion: Judaism

Curriculum Links:

R.E. Attainment Target 1: Learning about Religions
- Beliefs and teachings – describe religious beliefs and teachings and their importance.

R.E. Attainment Target 2: Learning from Religion
- Meanings and purpose – ask questions about the significant experiences of key figures from religions studied.

QCA R.E. Scheme of Work Reference
- 5C – Where did the Christian Bible come from?

National Literacy Strategy Reference
- Year 5, Term 3, Text 1 – investigate texts from different cultures.

Story Reference:
The Bible 1 Samuel, Chapters 16 – 18.
A Tapestry of Tales by Sandra Palmer and Elizabeth Breuilly (Collins Educational, 1993).
Stories from the Jewish World (MacDonald, 1988).
Storyteller Series: Jewish Stories by Anita Ganeri (Evans Brothers, 2001).
Modern World Religions: Judaism (Heinemann Educational Publishers, 2002).

Notes – Pages 29 and 30 – David the Shepherd Boy:

Introduction/Discussion:
- Discuss the wealth of detail in the Bible story, which shows us how unlikely it was that a young boy like David could defeat the giant.
- What does the Bible suggest was the reason for David's success?
- Discuss the extraordinary changes in David's life and expectations – from working as a shepherd boy for his father to becoming the King of Israel.
- Explain that the battle between David and Goliath is one of the most famous stories in the Old Testament. David is still a popular name around the world. There are many works of art showing David as a young hero, including the famous statue by Michelangelo.
- Discuss why a story about a small but brave person defeating a giant has remained so popular.

• 26 •

Notes – Page 31 – People of the Bible:

Introduction/Discussion:
- The six names in the box at the top of the page are key figures in the history of the Jewish people.
- Encourage children to see the connections between these people, reading the brief biographies together.
- Explain the significance of BCE (Before the Common Era). Explain that BCE dates should be read backwards.

Extension:
- Research and write brief biographies of some famous women from the Bible; e.g. Esther, Ruth, Mary, Deborah, Delilah.

Resources:
- Pencil or pen and crayons
- Bibles or Children's Bibles
- Non-fiction Christianity books for research
- Scissors, glue and paper
- ICT opportunity – use a computer with the Internet or CD–ROM encyclopaedia for research

Answers:
1. 2000 BCE: Abraham, son, sheep/ram. (Genesis, Chapters 13 – 26).
2. 1700 BCE: Joseph, coat, Egypt. (Genesis, Chapters 37 – 47).
3. 1250 BCE: Moses, basket, Commandments. (Exodus, Chapters 2 – 40).
4. 1030 BCE: Samuel, God, king. (1 Samuel, Chapters 1 – 16).
5. 1010 BCE: David, Samuel, Goliath. (1 Samuel, Chapter 16 and 1 Kings, Chapter 2).
6. 970 BCE: Solomon, Temple, Queen. (1 Kings, Chapters 1 – 11).

Notes – Page 32 – About David:

Introduction/Discussion:
- The Bible tells us a little about why David was chosen. When the prophet Samuel went to find the new king he thought it must be Jesse's son, Eliab. However, the Lord said, 'Pay no attention to how tall or handsome he is. I have rejected him, because I do not judge as people judge. They look at the outward appearance but I look at the heart'.

Extension:
- Read more about the life of David and make a collection of pictures and statues of him, using reference books and the Internet.

Resources:
- Pencil or pen and crayons
- Bibles
- Non-fiction books about David for research
- ICT opportunity – use a computer with the Internet or CD–ROM encyclopaedia for research

Answers:

Teacher check. Answers should demonstrate some awareness of David's life up to this point and be based upon the following verses from the Bible.

2. In the *Good News Bible,* 1 Samuel, Chapter 17, Verse 34, David tells Saul:
    'I take care of my father's sheep. Whenever a lion or a bear carries off a lamb, I go after it, attack it and rescue the lamb. If the lion or bear turns on me, I grab it by the throat and beat it to death. I have killed lions and bears and I will do the same to this heathen Philistine.'

4. David also strongly believes that God is on his side, and says to Goliath in Verse 45:
    'You are coming against me with sword, spear and javelin, but I come against you in the name of the Lord Almighty, the God of Israelite armies which you have defied. This very day the Lord will put you in my power.'

Notes – Page 33 – Psalm 23:

Introduction/Discussion:

*   The Book of Psalms contains 150 Psalms, about half of which are described as Psalms of David.
*   Psalm 23 is one of the best known Psalms of David. It has been set to music and is often sung during church services.
*   This version of Psalm 23 is taken from the Authorised or King James Bible of 1611.

Extension:

*   After working on the language used in Psalm 23, children could examine the language and images used in the King James versions of other Psalms; e.g. Psalms 8, 24 or 46.

Resources:

*   Pencil or pen and crayons
*   Bibles

Answers:

1. Teacher check. Possible answers include: maketh, pastures, leadeth, restoreth, righteousness, yea, thou, thy, staff, preparest, anointest, runneth, dwell.
2. The metaphor is a shepherd who provides fields of green grass for his sheep and a safe, calm water supply.
3. The *Good News Bible* translates these lines as:
    'Even if I go through the deepest darkness,
    I will not be afraid, Lord, for you are with me.'
4. (a) still = calm (b) dwell = live.

The Story of David the Shepherd Boy

Long ago in Bethlehem there lived a boy called David. One day, he was out in the fields near his home, looking after his father's sheep and practising some new tunes on his little harp. His father, Jesse, and his seven older brothers had all gone to meet the famous prophet, Samuel, so David was in charge of the flock.

Suddenly, he saw two of his sisters running towards him. Panting with excitement, they told him that he was needed down in the town. Samuel was here to anoint one of Jesse's sons as the next King of Israel. He had rejected Eliab, Abinadab and Shammah and their four younger brothers. Now he wanted to see David. Leaving his sisters in charge of the sheep, David hurried to Bethlehem. As soon as Samuel saw him, he knew that this young man would become the next king. He anointed him with oil as a sign that God would be with him.

Meanwhile, King Saul was suffering from an evil spirit. His servants had heard that Jesse's son was a fine musician so they suggested that he should come and play the harp to soothe the King. So David became one of the king's servants, playing music for him when he felt sad. When Saul did not need him, David continued to work for his father, watching over the sheep and defending them against lions and bears with his stick.

David's three older brothers were soldiers. They went with Saul's army to fight against a neighbouring tribe called the Philistines. The Philistines had a champion called Goliath, who was three metres tall. He carried a huge javelin and a vast spear with an iron point that weighed seven kilos. He wore heavy bronze armour on his chest and legs, and a great bronze helmet. Each morning, Goliath stood and shouted his challenge to Saul's army. He was calling for one champion from the Israelites to come and fight him. None of Saul's men dared to face this giant.

One day, Jesse asked David to go and visit his older brothers at the army camp in the valley of Elah, to take them some bread and cheese and bring back news. So David got up early the next morning, leaving someone else to take care of the sheep, and set off with the food. He arrived at the camp just as the Israelites were preparing for battle, shouting their war cries. He left the food with the supplies officer and ran to find his brothers. As they were talking, Goliath came forward from the Philistine line and called out his challenge again. The Israelites ran away in terror. Once they had reached safety, they explained to their young visitor that King Saul had promised a big reward to any man who could kill Goliath.

The Story of David the Shepherd Boy

The king had also promised to give the man his daughter's hand in marriage, and his family would have no more taxes to pay. Eliab, David's eldest brother, heard him asking about Goliath and was angry. He shouted 'What are you doing here? Who is taking care of those sheep of yours? You cheeky brat, coming here to watch us fight!'

Then King Saul heard that David was in the camp, and sent for him. David said to Saul, 'The army of the living God should not be afraid of this heathen Philistine. I will go and fight him'.

'No,' said Saul. 'You are just a boy, he is a soldier.'

Then David described what he had learned in his life as a shepherd: 'The Lord has saved me from lions and bears, he will save me from the Philistine'.

'Go, then,' said Saul, 'and the Lord be with you'. He offered David his own bronze helmet, armour and sword, but it was so heavy that the boy could not walk. Instead, David picked up his shepherd's stick and his leather sling, chose five smooth stones from a stream, and then walked forward to challenge Goliath.

When Goliath saw a slim young boy with no armour coming to fight him, he laughed loudly.

'What's the stick for? Do you think I am a dog? Come here, and I'll give your body to the birds.'

Then David answered, 'You have come here with a sword and a spear and a javelin, but I have come in the name of the Lord Almighty, the God of Israel. You have defied him, so I am going to cut off your head to show you the power of our God'.

Goliath started walking towards David with his spear ready, but David put a stone in his sling, swung it around then let it fly. The stone hit Goliath on the forehead and he fell down dead. Then David took Goliath's own sword out of its sheath and cut off his head. When the Philistines saw what had happened to their champion they ran away with the Israelite army chasing at their heels.

The people of Israel celebrated David's victory, but King Saul grew jealous because David was more popular than he was. He broke his promises and even tried to have David killed. But Saul's son, Jonathan, was a loyal friend to David. Jonathan saved David from Saul's plots.

Many years later, Saul and his sons were killed in battle. David the shepherd boy became king just as Samuel had prophesied. He was a great king and united the kingdoms of Judah and Israel.

People of the Bible

1. **Complete the first blank space in each description box, using the names below.**

   Moses   Samuel   Abraham   Solomon   David   Joseph

2. **Research and complete the rest of the spaces below.**

3. **Cut out each box and stick them on a time line, in chronological order.**

_____ was the favourite son of Jacob. He wore a special _____. His jealous brothers sold him as a slave. He went to _____, helped the king deal with a famine and was richly rewarded. Around 1700 BCE his father and brothers left Canaan and came to join him in Egypt.

_____ was the last of the great Judges of Israel. _____ called him when he was only a little boy. He led Israel for many years, then chose Saul to be the first _____, around 1030 BCE. After Saul's death, he anointed David to be king.

_____ was the son of King David and Queen Bathsheba. He became king around 970 BCE. There are many stories about his wisdom. He built the great _____ in Jerusalem and a magnificent palace for himself. The _____ of Sheba came to visit him.

_____ was born in Egypt. His mother hid him in a _____ and he was brought up by a princess. Around 1250 BCE the Israelites were living as slaves in Egypt. God called him to lead the people back to their promised land. He led his people through the wilderness and gave them the Ten _____.

_____ was called by God to be the founder of a great new nation. He left the city of Ur and travelled to Canaan around 2000 BCE. He was married to Sarah. God tested him to see if he was ready to sacrifice his _____, Isaac, but then sent a _____ instead.

_____ was a shepherd boy from Bethlehem, chosen by_____ as the future King of Israel. As a boy he killed the giant _____. Later, he fought bravely against his country's enemies. He became king when Saul died around 1010 BCE. He built his capital in Jerusalem.

About David

1.   Read the First Book of Samuel, Chapter 17, Verses 34 – 37.

2.   What did David learn as a shepherd, that helped him to fight Goliath?

_____

_____

_____

_____

_____

_____

_____

_____

3.   Read the First Book of Samuel, Chapter 17, Verses 45 – 47.

4.   How did David's faith in God help him to face Goliath?

_____

_____

_____

_____

_____

_____

_____

_____

Psalm 23 is traditionally a Psalm written by David.

Psalm 23

The Lord is my Shepherd; I shall not want.

He maketh me to lie down in green pastures:

He leadeth me beside the still waters.

He restoreth my soul:

He leadeth me in the paths of righteousness for his name's sake.

Yea, though I walk through the valley of the shadow of death,

I will fear no evil: for thou art with me;

Thy rod and thy staff they comfort me.

Thou preparest a table before me in the presence of mine enemies:

Thou anointest my head with oil;

My cup runneth over.

Surely goodness and mercy shall follow me all the days of my life:

And I shall dwell in the house of the Lord forever.

(This English translation dates from the early seventeenth century).

1. **Can you identify four words in Psalm 23 that are rarely used in modern English?**

    (a) _____ (b) _____

    (c) _____ (d) _____

2. **Explain the metaphor used in the first three lines.**

    _____

    _____

3. **Rewrite lines six and seven using modern English.**

    _____

    _____

4. **Explain what these words mean in the context of the psalm.**

    (a) still _____

    (b) dwell _____

Teacher Notes

Religion: Judaism

Curriculum Links:

R.E. Attainment Target 1: Learning about Religions
- Beliefs and teachings – describe religious beliefs and teachings and their importance.

R.E. Attainment Target 2: Learning from Religion
- Values and commitments – ask questions about matters of right and wrong and show understanding of moral and religious issues.

QCA R.E. Scheme of Work Reference
- 6C – Why are sacred texts important?

National Literacy Strategy Reference
- Year 6, Term 1, Text 6 – produce a modern retelling.

Story Reference:

The Bible, Exodus, Chapters 19 – 20.
A Tapestry of Tales by Sandra Palmer and Elizabeth Breuilly (Collins Educational, 1993).
Stories from the Jewish World (MacDonald, 1988).
Storyteller Series: Jewish Stories by Anita Ganeri (Evans Brothers, 2001).
Modern World Religions: Judaism (Heinemann Educational Publishers, 2002).

Notes – Pages 37 and 38 – How God gave Moses the Ten Commandments:

Introduction/Discussion:
- Examine how much detailed information the Bible gives us about exactly how and when Moses received the Commandments.
- What does this tell us about the importance of these words?
- The Bible includes more chapters of detailed rules that tell Jews how to live their lives, but the Ten Commandments are seen by both Jews and Christians as the most important Commandments.

Notes – Page 39 – Writing the Torah:

Introduction/Discussion:

- Discuss the skill of handwriting and the time and effort involved, compared with word processing on the computer.
- An average Torah scroll for synagogue use is about 60 metres long. It takes a trained scribe around 1000 working hours to complete.

Extension:

- Investigate how other faiths regard their sacred texts.
- Research how their sacred texts are treated during worship and at other times.

Resources:

- Pencil or pen and paper
- Clock or stopwatch
- Bibles
- Samples of Hebrew writing
- Pictures of a Torah being used during a service
- Pictures of other religious manuscripts; e.g. the Book of Kells
- Non-fiction Christianity books for research
- ICT opportunity – use a computer with the Internet or CD–ROM encyclopaedia for research

Answers:

1. Teacher check – one possible list is: h, e, b, d, i, j, c, f, a, g – however, accept any list which is logical and makes sense.
2. Teacher check.
3. Answers will vary, although the correct answer is 1 000 hours.
4. Teacher check.

Notes – Page 40 – My Rules for Life:

Introduction/Discussion:

- Discuss each of the Ten Commandments, using a clear, modern translation (or complete this activity after page 41 has been completed).
- Discuss whether the children consider each rule to be relevant to their own lives.
- Ensure the children are aware which forbidden activities are also illegal in a court of law.
- Compare the Ten Commandments with a list of school rules.

Extension:

- Compare these rules for life with others that the class may have encountered either in RE lessons or during family worship.
- Sort a list of rules from another faith into the same categories.

Resources:

- Pencil or pen and crayons
- Copy of the Ten Commandments (and/or completed page 41)

Answers:

(a) The sixth and eighth Commandments are against the law.
(b) Teacher check – most schools will ban the third, eighth, ninth and tenth Commandments.
(c) At home, children should respect the fifth Commandment. Some families will keep the first, second, third and fourth Commandments.

Notes – Page 41 – A Modern Retelling:

Introduction/Discussion:
- Read the Authorised Version text aloud, to help the class appreciate the quality of the writing.
- If the children have had any experience of Shakespeare's plays, they may be interested to know that the Authorised Version was produced during Shakespeare's lifetime. Do the children find Shakespeare's language easier to understand?
- Discuss whether it is more important for the Bible to sound impressive or be easy to understand.
- Ensure the children can identify unfamiliar parts of verbs, e.g. shalt.

Extension:
- Read Exodus, Chapter 20.
- Compare their translations to other translations.
- Write a similar modern retelling of another passage from the Bible or from Shakespeare.

Resources:
- Pencil or pen and paper.
- Bibles.
- Dictionaries.

Answers:
Teacher check.

How God gave Moses the Ten Commandments

Moses was a great leader of the Jewish people. He was born in Egypt, where his people were treated as slaves. With God's help, Moses persuaded the Egyptian ruler, the Pharaoh, to free the Jews and let them return to their own country.

After crossing the Red Sea and travelling across the desert for several weeks, Moses and the people of Israel reached the Sinai desert. They camped at the foot of Mount Sinai and Moses went up the mountain to speak to God. God told Moses to explain to the Israelites that it was their God who had brought them safely out of Egypt and now he wished to make them his chosen people. They must make the ritual preparations for worship then come to the foot of the mountain.

Three days later there was thunder and lightning. Mount Sinai was covered with a thick cloud, and the people could hear the sound of a trumpet coming from the mountain. God called Moses to come to the top of the mountain alone. There he told him the Ten Commandments and many other laws that he wanted Jews to follow.

Moses spent forty days and nights up in the clouds on top of Mount Sinai. He returned with not only the Ten Commandments but many other detailed instructions. Some of these laws told the Jews how to behave in their daily lives, how to treat other people, how to respect the Sabbath and what they could and could not eat. Other laws told them how and when they should worship their God, and even described the special box in which they should store the two stone tablets that God gave to Moses, on which God himself had written his Commandments.

But while Moses and Joshua were up on Mount Sinai, the people became very anxious and restless. They said they needed a god to worship so Aaron melted down all their earrings, poured the gold into a mould and created a golden calf. Then they sacrificed animals to this new god and held a drunken feast.

God saw this and was very angry, saying he would destroy the people of Israel. Moses pleaded with God to remember the promise he had made to Abraham, that one day he would have as many descendants as there are stars in the sky, and they would have land of their own.

How God gave Moses the Ten Commandments

Then Moses went down to the foot of the mountain and threw the stone tablets on the ground so that they broke. He melted down the golden calf, and punished the Israelites. God forgave the people, he gave them new stone tablets and made a contract with them as his chosen people.

The Israelites spent forty years wandering in the wilderness. Moses himself was not allowed to enter the promised land, only to look down on it from the mountains near Jericho. Then Moses died and Joshua led the people across the Jordan to their new home.

I am the Lord your God. Worship no God but me.

Do not make yourselves images of anything in heaven or on earth or in the water or under the earth. Do not bow down to any idol or worship it.

Do not use my name for evil purposes.

Observe the Sabbath and keep it holy.

Respect your father and your mother.

Do not commit murder.

Do not commit adultery.

Do not steal.

Do not accuse anyone falsely.

Do not desire another man's house, or anything that he owns.

Writing the Torah

1. **Read these sentences and number them in the correct order, so they make sense.**

    (a)   Exodus is the second book of the Bible.   ☐

    (b)   There are 250 columns of writing on a Torah scroll.   ☐

    (c)   Between services, Torah scrolls are stored in a special cupboard called the Ark.   ☐

    (d)   It takes about one thousand hours to copy the Torah onto a scroll.   ☐

    (e)   The Torah in a synagogue is always handwritten not printed.   ☐

    (f)   Genesis is the first book of the Bible.   ☐

    (g)   The story of God giving the Law to Moses is in the Book of Exodus.   ☐

    (h)   Jews call the first five books of the Bible the Torah.   ☐

    (i)   The Torah scrolls are the holiest objects in any synagogue.   ☐

    (j)   Torah scrolls are kept in a special box or wrapped in velvet.   ☐

2. **Copy the sentences above very carefully in your best handwriting, in the order you have chosen. If you make a mistake you will have to start again. Use a clock or stopwatch to see how long it takes you to write these 110 words.**

    I wrote 110 words in ☐ minutes and ☐ seconds.

3. **Look in a Bible at the books of Genesis, Exodus, Leviticus, Numbers and Deuteronomy. Estimate how many hours it would take a scribe to copy the books onto a Torah scroll.**

    I estimate it would take a scribe ☐ hours.

4. **Copy the Ten Commandments in your best handwriting, using the paper sideways. Attach a stick to either end and roll your work up, like a scroll.**

My Rules for Life

Read the Ten Commandments that God gave to Moses.

Write which rules you follow in your own life.

We follow the Commandments _____

_____

_____

_____

_____

_____ in the laws of our country.

We follow the Commandments _____

_____

_____

_____

_____

_____ in our school rules.

We follow the Commandments _____

_____

_____

_____

_____ in my home and family.

Write a list of the Commandments that you do not follow on the back.

Moses and the Ten Commandments – A Modern Retelling

This is the way the Ten Commandments are written in the Bible translation authorised by King James I in the early seventeenth century.

On a separate piece of paper, rewrite each Commandment in clear, modern English. You may need to use a dictionary.

I am the Lord the God, which brought thee out of the land of Egypt, from the house of bondage. Thou shalt have none other gods before me.

Thou shalt not make thee any graven image, or any likeness of any thing that is in heaven above, or that is in the earth beneath, or that is in the waters beneath the earth: thou shalt not bow down thyself unto them, or serve them.

Thou shalt not take the name of the Lord thy God in vain: for the Lord will not hold him guiltless that taketh his name in vain.

Keep the Sabbath day to sanctify it, as the Lord thy God hath commanded thee. Six days thou shalt labour, and do all thy work: but the seventh day is the Sabbath of the Lord thy God: in it thou shalt not do any work, thou, nor thy son, nor thy daughter, nor thy manservant, nor thy maidservant, nor thine ox, nor thine ass, nor any of thy cattle, nor thy stranger that is within thy gates; that thy manservant and thy maidservant may rest as well as thou.

Honour thy father and thy mother, as the Lord thy God hath commanded thee; that thy days may be prolonged, and that it may go well with thee, in the land which the Lord thy God giveth thee.

Thou shalt not kill.

Neither shalt thou commit adultery.

Neither shalt thou steal.

Neither shalt thou bear false witness against thy neighbour.

Neither shalt thou desire thy neighbour's wife, neither shalt thou covet thy neighbour's house, his field, or his manservant, or his maidservant, his ox, or his ass, or anything that is thy neighbour's.

Religion: Hinduism

Curriculum Links:

R.E. Attainment Target 1: Learning about Religions
- Practices and lifestyles – show understanding of ways of belonging to religions.
- Practices and lifestyles – show how religious beliefs can be expressed in a variety of forms.

R.E. Attainment Target 2: Learning from Religion
- Identity and experience – make informed responses to questions of identity and experience.

QCA R.E. Scheme of Work Reference
- 6F – How do people express faith through the arts?

National Literacy Strategy Reference
- Year 6, Term 1, Text 6 – manipulate narrative perspective by writing a story with two different narrators.
- Year 6, Term 1, Text 9 – prepare a short section of story as a script, using stage directions and location/setting.

Story Reference:
Out of the Ark by Anita Ganeri (Simon and Schuster Young Books, 1994).
A Tapestry of Tales by Sandra Palmer and Elizabeth Breuilly (Collins Educational, 1993).
Stories from the Hindu World (MacDonald, 1988).
Storyteller Series: Hindu Stories by Anita Ganeri (Evans Brothers, 2001).
Modern World Religions: Hinduism by Pat Wotten (Heinemann Educational Publishers, 2002).

Notes – Pages 45 and 46 – The Story of Princess Dayamati and the Five Kings:

Introduction/Discussion:
- Discuss how, in Hindu tradition, the gods are portrayed as being very closely involved with everyday human existence.
- What is the significance of the clues that Dayamati uses to identify her human lover among his supernatural competitors?
- Discuss how the gods abide by the rules and let Dayamati choose her own husband – unlike many of the gods in the Greek myths.

Extension:
- Compare this story with some fairytales and/or myths.

Notes – Page 47 – Hinduism and the Arts:

Introduction/Discussion:
- Discuss what we mean by 'the arts'.
- Which 'arts' subjects do the children study at school?
- How could the story of Dayamati be told through the arts? Which art form do the children think would tell the story most effectively?

Extension:
- Use non-fiction books or the Internet to find examples of Hindu art. Discuss the style and colours used.

Resources:
- Pencil or pen and crayons
- Non-fiction Hinduism books for research
- ICT opportunity – use a computer with the Internet or CD-ROM encyclopaedia for research

Answers:
1. Sita, Ravana, Hanuman, Lanka.
2. red, gold, white.
3. Navratri, nine, sticks.
4. Puja, avatars, Shiva.
   (NB: Many Hindu words have several, equally correct, spellings.)

Notes – Page 48 – Different Perspectives:

Introduction/Discussion:
- Read the story again.
- On the first half of the letter, focus upon the role of King Nala. Imagine King Nala's journey to meet Princess Dayamati. How does he feel when he meets the gods and Princess Dayamati?
- On the second half of the letter, focus upon the role of Princess Dayamati. Imagine Princess Dayamati's initial anxiety when making her choice. How does she spot the difference between King Nala and the gods? What does she rely on to pick the right man?

Extension:
- Give the version of events from a third character's view; e.g. Dayamati's father or one of the gods.

Resources:
- Pencil or pen and crayons

Answers:
Teacher check.

Notes – Page 49 – Princess Dayamati's Choice:

Introduction/Discussion:
- Read the section of the story that deals with Dayamati making her choice.
- Discuss the characters in this section: their motivation, personality, appearance and what they need to say.
- What does an Indian palace look like? Look at illustrations.
- Discuss and list the events that take place during this important scene.
- Look at plays, examine how they differ from stories.
- List the differences in organisation: no speech marks, no use of words like 'said', each person's speech presented separately, inclusion of stage directions.

Extension:
- Write a script for the entire story, add extra characters or invent a new scene.
- Groups of children could perform the 'best' scripts, either in the classroom or for a larger audience.

Resources:
- Pencil or pen
- Story of Princess Dayamati and the Five Kings
- Selection of plays
- Pictures of Indian palaces
- Lined paper to continue writing script on

Answers:
Cast list: King Bhima, Princess Dayamati, King Nala, Indra, Varuna, Agni and Yama.
Setting and Script: Teacher check.

The Story of Princess Dayamati and the Five Kings

The Story of Princess Dayamati and the Five Kings

Hinduism and the Arts

Hindus in India and around the world make great use of the arts to express their ancient and complex faith.

Use reference books to help you complete the following.

Hindus use drama to tell the story of how Rama's wife, _____, was kidnapped by the demon _____. The god _____ helped Rama to rescue her from the island of _____.

Hindu women choose special colours at different times in their lives. A Hindu bride's sari is always _____ and _____. Traditionally, a widow wears _____.

At the festival of _____ , Hindus dance for _____ nights. The dancers use special _____ for the dance called *dandia ras.*

In Hindu temples and homes you will find elaborate images of the gods, used for private worship or _____. Hindus believe Vishnu has come to earth many times in different forms or_____. _____ the destroyer is often shown like this in the dance of the universe.

Different Perspectives

1. Imagine you are the real King Nala. Write a short letter to a friend describing your journey to the palace and meeting the gods and Princess Dayamati for the first time.

_____

_____

_____

_____

_____

_____

_____

_____

_____

_____

_____

_____

2. Imagine you are Princess Dayamati. Continue King Nala's letter, explaining how you chose the right man to be your husband.

_____

_____

_____

_____

_____

_____

_____

_____

_____

_____

_____

_____

Princess Dayamati's Choice

Write your own script for the scene at the palace where King Bhima tells Princess Dayamati to choose her husband and she sees five King Nalas. List the cast and describe the setting. Remember to include stage directions to help your performers.

Cast List: • _____

 • _____

 • _____

 • _____

 • _____

 • _____

 • _____

Setting: _____

_____

King Bhima: *(Smiling)* Welcome to my palace, my friends, on this very special day.

_____

_____

_____

_____

_____

_____

_____

_____

_____

_____

_____

_____

_____

_____

_____

_____

_____

Teachers Notes

Religion: Hinduism

Curriculum Links:

R.E. Attainment Target 1: Learning about Religions
- Beliefs and teachings - explain how some beliefs and teachings are shared by different religions and how they make a difference to the lives of individuals and communities.

R.E. Attainment Target 2: Learning from Religion
- Values and commitments - make informed responses to people's values and commitments (including religious ones) in the light of their learning.

QCA R.E. Scheme of Work Reference
- 6C - Why are sacred texts important?

National Literacy Strategy Reference
- Year 6, Term 2, Sentence 1 - investigate the use of active and passive verbs.
- Year 6, Term 2, Word 5 - investigate word roots.

Story Reference:
Seasons of Splendour by Madhur Jaffrey (Pavilion, 1985).
A Tapestry of Tales by Sandra Palmer and Elizabeth Breuilly (Collins Educational, 1993).
Stories from the Hindu World (MacDonald, 1988).
Storyteller Series: Hindu Stories by Anita Ganeri (Evans Brothers, 2001).
Modern World Religions: Hinduism by Pat Wotten (Heinemann Educational Publishers, 2002).
Hindu Scriptures by V.P. Kanitkar (Heinemann, 1994).

Notes – Pages 53 and 54 – The Birth of Krishna:

Introduction/Discussion:
- The story of Krishna is told in the ancient Hindu epic poem the Mahabharata, which has 110 000 couplets, each of which is 32 syllables long. The Mahabharata is divided into eighteen separate books. The many variations in style and content suggest that it was not the work of a single author. The ancient texts were collected together later, probably between 300 BCE and 300 CE.
- Originally handwritten in Sanskrit, the Mahabharata was later translated into Hindi and Tamil. The text was first printed in Calcutta in the 1830s and was translated into English in the 1890s.
- According to Hindu texts, the god Vishnu has come to earth many times with different identities or avatars. King Rama, whose story is told in the Ramayana, was one of these avatars and the god Krishna was another.

Notes – Pages 55 and 56 – Sacred Texts:

Introduction/Discussion:
- Read and discuss the questions with the class, ensuring that children know which questions relate to which faith and sacred text.

Extension:
- Compile a quiz for their classmates, based on both their research and knowledge of their own faith.

Resources:
- Pencil or pen
- Sacred texts, encyclopaedias and non-fiction books about the six major world religions
- ICT opportunity – use a computer with the Internet or CD-rom encyclopaedia for research
  (NB: All answers can be found on the Encarta CD-ROM.)

Answers:
The Christian Bible:
1. (a) Matthew (b) Mark (c) Luke (d) John
2. Greek
3. Revelation:
   The Authorised Version is entitled *The Revelation of St. John the Divine*.
   The Good News Bible is entitled *The Revelation to John*.
4. St Paul
5. A lectern is a reading desk used in churches to hold a Bible. It is often shaped like an eagle with outspread wings. People stand at the lectern during services to read from the Bible.

The Muslim Qur'an:
1. 7th Century CE
2. Arabic
3. Gabriel
4. Suras
5. (a) 2nd (b) 114th

Sacred Hindu Texts:
1. Four
2. Sanskrit
3. The Pandavas and Kauravas
4. Rama
5. Sita is kidnapped by the demon Ravana and taken to the island of Lanka.

The Jewish Torah:
1. The Law or instruction
2. (a) Genesis (b) Exodus (c) Leviticus (d) Numbers (e) Deuteronomy
3. In a special cupboard or alcove called the Ark
4. Hebrew
5. Genesis

Sacred Buddhist Texts:
1. Three baskets
2. Buddha
3. Vinaya Pitaka
4. Sanskrit, Pali, Tibetan, Chinese
5. Four

The Sikh Guru Granth Sahib:
1. The eleventh – Guru Granth Sahib
2. Punjabi
3. 48 hours
4. Remove shoes, cover head and bow
5. The book is opened at random and the baby is given a name beginning with the first letter at the top of the page.

Notes – Page 57 – Active and Passive Verbs:

Introduction/Discussion:
- This worksheet is intended for use after class work on active and passive verbs.
- Re-read part of the story and discuss whether each verb used is active or passive.

Extension:
- After children have identified the active and passive verbs in the story of Krishna, they could go on to analyse another piece of text from a fiction book, then make lists of the active and passive verbs used.

Resources:
- Pencil or pen
- Story *The Birth of Krishna*
- Dictionaries
- Fiction books

Answers:
1. (a), (d) and (f)
2. Teacher check
3. (a) AQUA means water in Latin.
   (b) PHOTO means light in Greek.
   (c) TELE means distant in Greek.
4. Teacher check, but answers could include:
   (a) AQUA: Aquarius, aquatic, aquatint, aquaerobics, aquaplane
   (b) PHOTO: photographer, photocopier, photofit, photogenic
   (c) TELE: telegram, telepathy, telecommunications, Teletext

The Story of the Birth of Krishna

Long ago in India, by the Yamuna river, there lived a cruel and wicked prince called Kans. He put his own father in prison and made himself King of Mathura.

Kans had a sister called Devaki, a kind girl who loved her husband, Vasudev, very much. Not long after their wedding, a wise old man approached King Kans and told him that one day he was fated to die at the hands of Devaki's child. Kans was angry, and wanted to get rid of his sister at once, but everyone around her loved her so much for her goodness that he did not dare execute her.

Instead, Kans put his sister and her new husband into a prison cell together, and there she gave birth to a daughter. When the prison guards told the king, he rushed to the cell, picked up his sister's baby and threw her onto the stone floor. Her spirit rose up to heaven and a voice called, 'You evil man, my brother is coming to kill you!'

Years passed. Devaki and Vasudev had six more baby daughters in their prison cell. All were killed by their wicked uncle and died calling, 'You evil man, my brother is coming to kill you!'

Finally the great god Vishnu, protector of the universe, saw that it was time for him to come to Mathura. Vishnu can appear in many forms, as a fish or a lion, as a warrior or as Rama. This time, Vishnu came in the shape of the god Krishna and was born on a stormy August night as Devaki's eighth child.

As soon as the baby was born, Vasudev heard a voice telling him to carry the baby across the river to be cared for in Gokula, by Yashoda and Nanda. 'But our cell is locked, there are guards on duty, and the river water is so high,' said Vasudev. 'Don't worry,' said the voice. 'Take the baby to your sister and be back by dawn and all will be well.'

So Devaki wrapped her son up warmly and kissed him goodbye, then Vasudev picked him up and pushed the cell door. It opened, and there were the guards, all fast asleep. He went out into the night and walked through the storm into the river. The water was deep and flowing fast because of the monsoon rains but Vasudev bravely stepped into the water and started to cross.

At first, as he waded through the Yamuna, he carried the baby in his arms, but the water rose so he lifted him onto his shoulders. The water kept rising so he put the baby on his head. The water was now almost filling his nostrils, and Vasudev thought he would have to turn back. Then the baby Krishna reached down with one tiny foot and dipped his toe in the water. At once the flood waters of the Yamuna calmed, and Vasudev was able to walk to the opposite bank. Krishna knew that the waters had risen only in order to reach him, so he stilled the waters for his father with that one touch.

Soon, Vasudev reached his sister's house where Yashoda and her husband, Nanda, were happy to see him and promised to take good care of the baby Krishna. Vasudev hurried back to tell Devaki that her baby was safe.

When King Kans discovered that the baby was gone he was furious. He killed all the baby boys in Mathura, but he did not find Krishna, for he was on the other side of the river, outside the kingdom.

The Story of the Birth of Krishna

Krishna grew up happily in Gokula with his aunt and uncle, playing with his cousin, Balram, and helping to take care of the cattle. He became famous among the cowherds, defeating a demon sent by King Kans and saving the people of the village from a great river serpent.

When King Kans heard that his nephew was still alive he remembered the old man's warning and plotted to bring Krishna to his court so he could kill him. He had heard that Krishna and Balram were keen wrestlers, so he announced that he would hold a great wrestling championship at his court. He sent messengers to all the neighbouring kingdoms offering a huge prize to any young men who could stand up to his two giant fighters, Chanur and Mustik.

Krishna and Balram hurried to the palace of Mathura, eager to try their strength against the champions. But King Kans had no intention of letting his nephew win in a fair fight. He wanted to see Krishna dead.

The crowd cheered when Krishna and Balram walked into the ring and stood waiting to face the king's champion wrestlers. But instead, King Kans gave the signal for his men to release a huge wild elephant. Everyone gasped as the elephant charged towards them

with its huge feet and sharp tusks, but Krishna leaped onto its back, grabbed the elephant by the neck and held on until the elephant fell dead.

King Kans could barely hide his anger as the crowd cheered. He summoned his two wrestlers, Chanur and Mustik, and ordered them to finish off these two young men. Confident of victory, the two enormous champions strolled into the ring. Krishna called to his cousin, 'You take Mustik, I can mange Chanur'. Krishna tackled Chanur by the neck, Balram grabbed Mustik in a bear hug and within minutes both the king's champions lay dead on the ground.

As King Kans sat screaming for his soldiers to defend him, Krishna ran across and lifted his uncle off the throne, shouting, 'You evil man, you killed my sisters and now I have come to kill you!'

As soon as the evil Kans was dead, Krishna hurried to the prison where his parents and his grandfather had been kept for so long. Devaki and Vasudev were delighted to see their son and to hear that the prophesy had come true. Krishna's grandfather, the rightful king, took back his throne and ruled wisely to make Mathura a happy place again.

 Prim-Ed Publishing – www.prim-ed.com

Sacred Texts 1

Research and answer these questions on Christian, Muslim and Hindu texts.

The Christian Bible

1. What are the names of the Gospels?

    (a) _____ (b) _____

    (c) _____ (d) _____

2. Which language was used to write the Gospels? _____

3. What is the last book of the Bible called? _____

4. Who wrote letters to the people of Rome, Corinth and Ephesus? _____

5. In church, what is the purpose of a lectern? _____

    _____

    _____

The Muslim Qur'an

1. In which century was the Qur'an written? _____

2. Which language is used in the Qur'an? _____

3. Which angel dictated the Qur'an to Muhammad? _____

4. What are the 114 chapters of the Qur'an called? _____

5. Which are the longest and shortest chapters of the Qur'an?

    (a) Longest: _____ (b) Shortest: _____

Sacred Hindu Texts

1. How many Vedas are there? _____

2. What is the language used in the Vedas? _____

3. Which two groups are at war in the Mahabharata? _____

4. Who is the hero of the Ramayana? _____

5. What happens to the hero's wife? _____

    _____

    _____

Research and answer these questions on Jewish, Buddhist and Sikh texts.

The Jewish Torah

1. What does the word Torah mean? _____

2. What are the names of the five books that form the Torah?

    (a) _____ (b) _____

    (c) _____ (d) _____ (e) _____

3. Where is the Torah kept in a synagogue? _____
    _____

4. Which language is used in the Torah? _____

5. Which book tells the story of Adam and Eve? _____

Sacred Buddhist Texts

1. What is the meaning of Tripitaka? _____

2. The Sutra Pitaka records whose conversations? _____

3. Which Pitaka gives rules for Buddhist monks and nuns?_____

4. Name some of the languages used in Buddhist texts._____

5. How many Noble Truths did Buddha describe? _____

The Sikh Guru Granth Sahib

1. The Sikh holy book is honoured as which guru? _____

2. Which language is used in the Granth Sahib? _____

3. How many hours does it take to read the whole book in an Akhand Path? _____

4. What should a Sikh do when coming into the room where the book is kept?_____
    _____

5. How does the Granth Sahib help a Sikh family choose a name for a new baby? _____
    _____

Active and Passive Verbs

1. **Draw a circle around the three sentences which contain active verbs.**

    (a) Kans put the king in prison.   (b) The king was imprisoned.

    (c) The baby was saved.   (d) Vasudev saved the baby.

    (e) The wild elephant was released.   (f) The men released the wild elephant.

2. **Find three examples of phrases with active verbs in the story of the birth of Krishna. Copy them here. Write the phrases again, changing the verbs to passive verbs.**

    (a) _____

        _____

    (b) _____

        _____

    (c) _____

        _____

3. **Use a dictionary to find the meanings of these words.**

    | aquarium | aqualung | aqueduct | aquamarine |

    (a) Aqua means _____

    | photograph | photocopy | telephoto | photosynthesis |

    (b) Photo means _____

    | television | telephone | telegraph | telescope |

    (c) Tele means _____

4. **Write other words which use the roots: aqua–, photo– and tele–.**

aqua–	photo–	tele–

Religion: Islam

Curriculum Links:

R.E. Attainment Target 1: Learning about Religions

- Beliefs and teachings – explain how some beliefs and teachings are shared by different religions and how they make a difference to the lives of individuals and communities.

R.E. Attainment Target 2: Learning from Religion

- Meaning and purpose – ask questions about the significant experiences of key figures from religions studied.

QCA R.E. Scheme of Work Reference

- 5A – Why is Muhammad important to Muslims?

National Literacy Strategy Reference

- Year 5, Term 1, Word 7 – explain differences between synonyms and shades of meaning.

Story Reference:

The earliest version of the life of Muhammad was written by Ibu Ishaq one hundred years after Muhammad died.
The stories of Muhammad's life are known as the Hadith. Modern accounts include:
The Life of Muhammad by Alfred Guillaume (OUP, 1987).
Muhammad for Beginners by Sardat and Malik (Cambridge Icon Books, 1994).
Leaders of Religion: Muhammad by Dilwyn Hunt (Oliver and Boyd, 1996).
Themes in Religion by Alan Brine (Longman, 1991).
Muhammad: His Life Based on the Earliest Sources by Martin Lings (Islamic Texts Society, 1993).
A Tapestry of Tales by Sandra Palmer and Elizabeth Breuilly (Collins Educational, 1993).
Stories from the Muslim World (MacDonald, 1988).
Storyteller Series: Muslim Stories by Anita Ganeri (Evans Brothers, 2001).
Modern World Religions: Islam (Heinemann Educational Publishers, 2002).

Notes – Pages 61 and 62 – The Early Life of Muhammad:

Introduction/Discussion:

- Discuss what the children already know about the prophet Muhammad and his importance to Muslims.
- Discuss why Mecca is important and what the Ka'ba is.
- Explain that many Muslims will write or say the words 'Peace be unto him' every time they use the name Muhammad.
- After reading the story, discuss the supernatural elements. What message do the supernatural elements give to Muslims?

Notes – Page 63 – What is the Message?:

Introduction/Discussion:

- What is important about each story?
- Muslims describe Muhammad as the Messenger of God. How does each story help us to see Muhammad as someone special?
- How could these stories help Muslims to understand the teachings of the Qur'an and put them into practice in their own lives?

Extension:

- Read other stories about the early life of Muhammad and consider their significance.

Resources:

- Pencil or pen and crayons
- Books about the early life of Muhammad for research

Answers:

(a) When the angels looked at Muhammad's heart and washed it with snow it showed that he was already someone very special who would grow up with a pure heart.

(b) When the old monk saw the cloud and the tree shading Muhammad from the sun he saw this as a sign that the boy was someone of great spiritual importance, the prophet who would come to the Arabs.

(c) When Muhammad was asked to choose who would have the honour of putting the sacred stone back in its place he showed wisdom in the way he solved the argument. He allowed all of the workers to share in lifting the cloth that supported the stone.

Notes – Page 64 – The Five Pillars of Islam:

Introduction/Discussion:

- Read about the five basic elements of Islam and discuss their significance with the class.
- Remind children of similar elements in other faiths that they may have studied.
- Ask children who follow other faiths whether they can relate any aspects of the Pillars of Islam to the practice of their own faith.

Extension:

- The worksheet provides space for children to compare each of the Pillars of Islam with a practice from two other faiths. Children could also research and record information from a wider range of faiths on a separate sheet.

Resources:

- Pencil or pen
- Non-fiction books about major world religions
- ICT opportunity – use a computer with the Internet or CD–ROM encyclopaedia for research

Answers:

Teacher check – answers may include the following:
- Declaration of Faith: Christian creeds, Jewish Shema.
- Prayer: Jews pray three times a day, Hindus offer puja daily, Christian monks and nuns pray throughout the day, regular prayer is also important for Sikhs and Buddhists.
- Charity: Sikhs offer food to all, many Christian-based charities help the poor.
- Fasting: Christians traditionally limit their diet during Lent, Jews have three fasting days during the year.
- Pilgrimage: Buddhists visit Buddha's birthplace at Lumbini, Sikhs visit the temple at Amritsar, Hindus visit the River Ganges, Jews visit Jerusalem, Christians visit shrines like Lourdes and Canterbury.

Notes – Page 65 – Synonyms:

Introduction/Discussion:
- Define what a synonym is.
- Think of synonyms for a selection of words: happy, funny, miserable etc.
- Complete questions 1(a) and (b) from the worksheet orally.
- Discuss which word seems most appropriate in each context.
- Stress that there may be more than one correct answer to these questions.
- Model the use of dictionaries and thesauruses to help find synonyms and therefore improve vocabulary.

Extension:
- Use the dictionaries and thesauruses to find other sets of words with similar meanings.

Resources:
- Pencil or pen and crayons
- Dictionaries
- Thesauruses

Answers:
1. Teacher check - there is more than one correct answer to these questions. However, the 'best' answers would be:
   (a) astonished
   (b) tragic
   (c) exhausted
   (d) wise
   (e) arguing
2. Teacher check - there are many different answers to these questions. Answers might include:
   (a) handsome, attractive, pretty, beautiful, lovely
   (b) rich, wealthy, prosperous, fortunate, affluent, well-off
   (c) angry, frustrated, cross, annoyed, upset

The Early Life of Muhammad

Muslims tell many stories about the early life of their great prophet, Muhammad.

Muhammad was born around the year 570 BCE in Mecca, in the country now known as Saudi Arabia. His father died before he was born, and his mother, Amina, sent him into the desert to be cared for by a foster mother, Halimah.

One day, when Muhammad was still a very young child, his foster mother had sent him outside to play near their tents with her own son. Suddenly, her child came running in, to tell her that two men in white had taken Muhammad, opened up his chest and put their hands inside.

Halimah and her husband ran to see and found Muhammad standing unhurt, but looking pale and shocked. There was no sign of the men in white, and no trace of any blood or wound on Muhammad's chest, but the two boys insisted that they were telling the truth.

Later in life Muhammad himself described what had happened, and how two angels all in white carrying a golden basin full of snow had opened up his chest, and pulled out his heart. They looked into his heart and took out a black clot of blood, then washed his heart with snow and put it back inside him.

A few years later Muhammad's mother, Amina, died, so he was then brought up by his uncle, Abu Talib. When Muhammad was about twelve his uncle took him with him to Syria as part of a caravan of merchants.

As they travelled home again, there was a long line of heavily laden camels and people making their way through the desert, under a blazing sun, towards Bostra. An old monk called Bahira lived there, guarding a collection of old manuscripts, some of which predicted that a great prophet would come to the Arabs. As Bahira watched the caravan approach he saw something extraordinary. A small, low cloud was floating just above the line of people, keeping the sun off just one or two travellers. Even stranger, when the whole caravan stopped to rest under a tree the cloud stopped too, and then the branches of the tree leaned over to shelter this same group from the hot midday sun.

Bahira was sure that these strange events were significant. He sent a message over to the travellers inviting them all to join him for a meal. They were happy to accept, but Abu Talib asked Muhammad, as the youngest in the group, to stay behind with the camels and keep an eye on the baggage.

When the travellers arrived at the monk's cell, Bahira looked closely at them all, but could see no sign of anyone that fitted the description in his manuscripts, nor seemed worthy of the wonders he had seen.

'Are you sure everyone is here?' he asked, 'I did invite all of you.'

'We've only left one boy behind,' they answered. 'He's over there with the camels.'

The Early Life of Muhammad

'Bring him,' urged Bahira. So they fetched Muhammad to join them, and as soon as Bahira saw his face he knew that this was the one whom the cloud and the tree had been sheltering. After questioning him for a few minutes, he turned to Abu Talib asking, 'What is your relationship to this boy?'

'He is my son,' replied Abu Talib.

'Surely not,' exclaimed Bahira. 'This boy's father is dead.'

'It is true,' Abu Talib agreed, 'I love him like my own, but he is my dead brother's son.'

'Then take him home and look after him,' warned the old man. 'Great things lie ahead for your brother's son.'

When Muhammad grew up he became a merchant himself and married a wealthy widow called Khadijah. He was respected by everyone who knew him, for his kindness and his wisdom.

In the centre of Mecca there was an old shrine called the Ka'ba. The most holy part of the shrine was a black stone built into one corner. It was said to have come from Paradise and been given to Abraham by an angel. The shrine was in a poor state, so the warring local clans agreed to work together and restore it.

They demolished the building down to its ancient foundations then rebuilt the stone walls and put on a wooden roof. All that remained was for the holy black stone to be lifted back into its special corner.

Each of the clans felt that they deserved the honour of replacing the stone, so there was a violent disagreement over who should finish the task. Work stopped altogether for several days and the rival groups were almost coming to blows. Then the oldest man on the site suggested that they let the next person to come to the shrine make the decision for them.

Moments later, in walked Muhammad, just home from a journey. He was already famous as a wise and humane judge, so all the clans agreed to abide by his decision.

As soon as they had explained the problem to Muhammad, he called for a cloak and carefully laid the sacred stone in the middle. Then he called upon all the workers to take hold of the edges of the cloak and together they lifted the stone up to the right height so that Muhammad himself could guide it back into its rightful place.

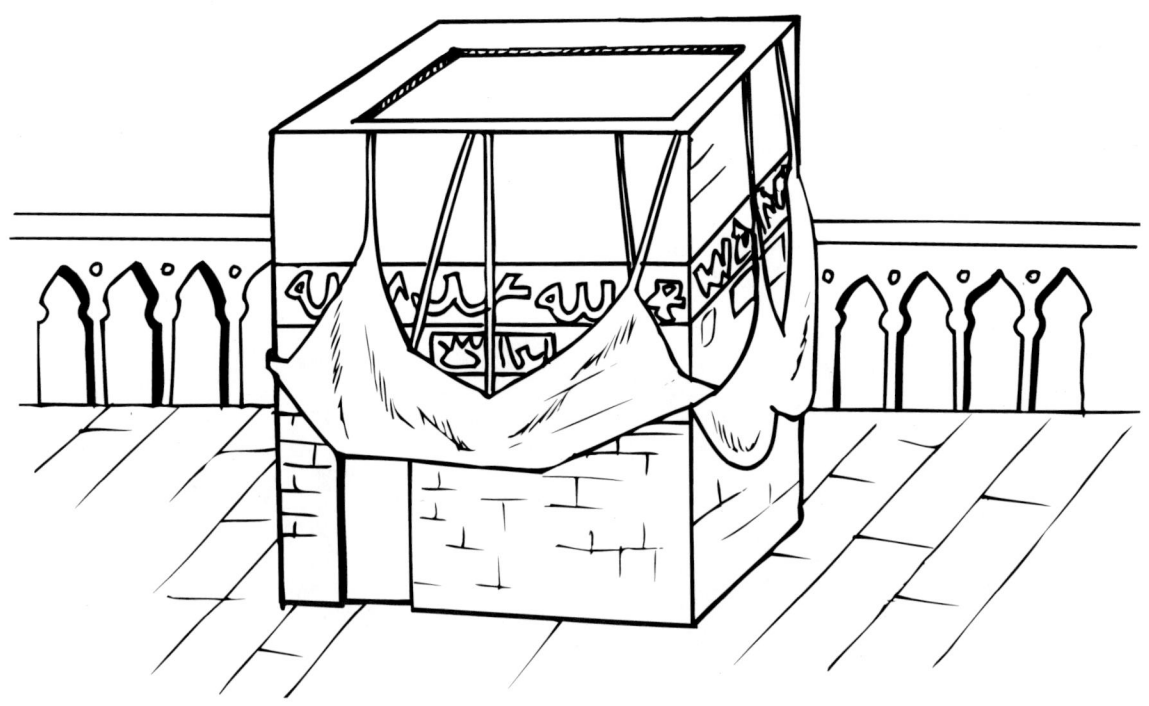

What is the Message?

In his adult life, Muhammad became an important prophet and also a very wise man. These three stories about Muhammad's early life show that there was already something special about him.

Write the message for Muslims behind each story.

1. The angels who looked at Muhammad's heart.

    _____

    _____

    _____

    _____

    _____

    _____

2. The cloud and tree that sheltered Muhammad from the sun.

    _____

    _____

    _____

    _____

    _____

    _____

3. Muhammad replacing the black stone in the Ka'ba.

    _____

    _____

    _____

    _____

    _____

    _____

The Five Pillars of Islam

Muhammad taught the first Muslims about the Five Pillars of Islam.

Other faiths make similar demands of their followers.

Research and compare two other faiths to complete the table.

Declaration of Faith	Prayer	Charity	Fasting	Pilgrimage
Shahadah: Muslims must make a declaration of faith.	Salaat: Muslims must pray five times a day.	Zakaat: Muslims must give to charity.	Sawm: Muslims must fast during the month of Ramadan.	Haj: Muslims must make a pilgrimage to Mecca.

A synonym is a word with a similar meaning to another word.

1. Circle the word that you think fits the best.

   (a) When Muhammad said he had seen two angels, his family were

surprised	astonished	flabbergasted	puzzled	astounded

   (b) The death of Muhammad's mother was

unfortunate	sad	tragic	disastrous	sorrowful

   (c) Walking through the desert, the people felt

fatigued	sleepy	weary	exhausted	tired

   (d) The old man, Bahira, was

wise	knowledgeable	learned	clever	intelligent

   (e) The different groups rebuilding the Ka'ba were

fighting	disagreeing	arguing	discussing	disputing

2. Write four synonyms to describe:

   (a) a good looking person.

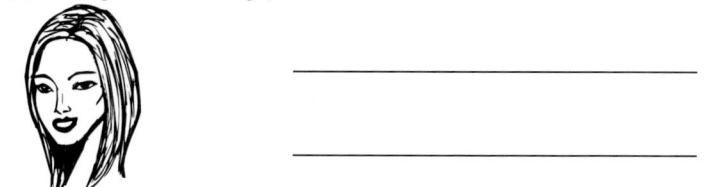

   _____   _____

   _____   _____

   (b) someone who has a lot of money.

   _____   _____

   _____   _____

   (c) how you feel when things go wrong for you.

   _____   _____

   _____   _____

Religion: Islam

Curriculum Links:

R.E. Attainment Target 1: Learning about Religions

- Practices and lifestyles - explain how selected features of religious life and practice make a difference to the lives of individuals and communities.

R.E. Attainment Target 2: Learning from Religion

- Values and commitments - make informed responses to people's values and commitments.

QCA R.E. Scheme of Work Reference

- 6D - What is the Qur'an and why is it important to Muslims?

National Literacy Strategy Reference

- Year 6, Term 1, Text 15 - develop a journalistic style.

Story Reference:

The earliest version of the life of Muhammad was written by Ibu Ishaq one hundred years after Muhammad died.

The stories of Muhammad's life are known as the Hadith. Modern accounts include:

The Life of Muhammad by Alfred Guillaume (OUP, 1987).

Muhammad for Beginners by Sardat and Malik (Cambridge Icon Books, 1994).

Notes – Pages 69 and 70 – The Night of Power:

Introduction/Discussion:

- Discuss the reverence Muslims show when handling copies of the Qur'an. It is always kept safely on a high shelf, never on the floor and devout Muslims wash their hands before touching the book.
- Does the story of the revelation to Muhammad help us to understand why Muslims treat the Qur'an with such respect?

Notes – Page 71 – How Much do You Know about Muslims?:

Extension:

- Children who are already well informed about the Islamic world could undertake a personal research project on a topic of interest, or write additional questions for their classmates.

Resources:

- Pencil or pen
- Non-fiction books about Islam for research
- ICT opportunity – use a computer with the Internet or CD-ROM encyclopaedia for research

Answers:

1. (c) All over the world
2. (c) A crescent moon with a star
3. (a) Muhammad went to Medina
4. (a) Visit Mecca once during their lifetime
5. (b) Eat only in the hours of darkness
6. (c) When they are about five years old
7. (a) Dress modestly
8. (b) Five times a day
9. (b) Pork and (d) Alcohol
10. (c) Brazil

Notes – Page 72 – The Name of God:

Introduction/Discussion:

- Muslims say there are 99 beautiful names for Allah, of which compassionate and merciful are the most important.
- Brainstorm synonyms for compassionate and merciful.
- Remind children of vocabulary used in other religions to praise God; e.g. in hymns.
- Remind children how to use dictionaries and thesauruses to increase their vocabulary.
- Show children examples of Islamic calligraphy and decoration.

Extension:

- Copy examples of Islamic calligraphy from books.

Resources:

- Pencil or pen and crayons
- Dictionaries
- Thesauruses
- Books containing Islamic calligraphy and decoration

Answers:

1. Teacher check - answers may include the following: good, tender, loving, gentle, sympathetic, benevolent, kind-hearted, charitable, lenient, understanding, beautiful, generous, bounteous, magnanimous, clement, patient, benign, indulgent
2. Teacher check

Notes – Page 73 – Mecca Times:

Introduction/Discussion:
- Re-read the story *The Night of Power.*
- Discuss which parts of the story are the most 'newsworthy'.
- Decide on the key elements of the story that must be included in the article.
- Decide whether this article is intended for a serious broadsheet newspaper or a sensational tabloid.
- Remind children not to draw Muhammad or the angel in their newspaper photograph space.
- Look at some broadsheet and tabloid newspaper articles for ideas about how a modern journalist would cover such a story.

Extension:
- Select and retell other stories from the life of Muhammad in the same style.
- Experiment by telling the same story in the style of different newspapers.

Resources:
- Pencil or pen and crayons.
- *The Night of Power* story.
- Broadsheet and tabloid newspaper articles of the same event

Answers:
Teacher check

The Night of Power

When Muhammad grew up he became a successful merchant in the city of Mecca. Like many people at that time he could neither read nor write, but he was trusted as an honest and hard working man. He worked for a wealthy widow called Khadijah, taking charge of her camels as they carried goods to market. Later he married her, and they had a large family with four daughters, Zainab, Ruqaiyyah, Umm Kulthum and Fatimah, and two sons who died young. Muhammad and Khadijah also took into their household a young cousin called Ali and a boy called Zaid.

Muhammad was a pious man so when he wanted to pray quietly and meditate he would leave their busy family house and spend a few nights in the hills nearby, in a cave he had found up on Mount Hira.

One night towards the end of the month of Ramadan, in the year 610 CE, when Muhammad was about forty years old, Muhammad was alone in the cave when suddenly an angel appeared and spoke to him. The angel held out a silk scroll with letters of fire and ordered him, 'Read'.

'I cannot,' replied Muhammad. Three times the angel ordered him to read the scroll, and the third time Muhammad looked, he found that he could read the Arabic words that were written on the scroll.

'Read, in the name of your Lord the Creator,

Who created mankind from a clot of blood.

Read, for your Lord is the most bountiful.

He has taught with the pen,

Teaching man that which he knew not.'

Muhammad read the words out loud to the angel. Muhammad told people afterwards that having read those words for the first time, he felt as though they were written on his heart and he could never forget them.

As the astonished Muhammad walked away from the cave towards home, trembling with shock, he heard the angel calling him, 'Muhammad, you are the Messenger of God, I am the angel Gabriel'.

Muhammad hurried back to tell Khadijah what had happened to him and repeat the angel's words. Khadijah, Ali and Zaid listened and believed the message Muhammad brought to the household and so these four people became the very first Muslims. Today there are millions of Muslims all over the world, and many of them have chosen these names taken from Muhammad's own family.

Soon afterwards, the Angel Gabriel returned to Muhammad and spoke to him again. Muhammad continued to receive revelations from God for the rest of his life. Muhammad began to preach in public and tell the people of Mecca about the wonderful message that he had received.

Muslims believe that the 114 suras that are now known as the Qur'an are not the work of any human author but are the word of God dictated to Muhammad by Gabriel. The Qur'an guides Muslims in all aspects of their lives. It was the angel who showed Muhammad how Muslims should wash themselves before their five daily prayers, and the positions they should use when they pray.

Muslims today remember the night when the Angel Gabriel first appeared to Muhammad in the cave on Mount Hira. They celebrate during the last ten days of the holy month of Ramadan, and particularly on the 27th day. Some believers stay awake all night praying and reciting the Qur'an. The festival is called Lailatul Qadr – the Night of Power.

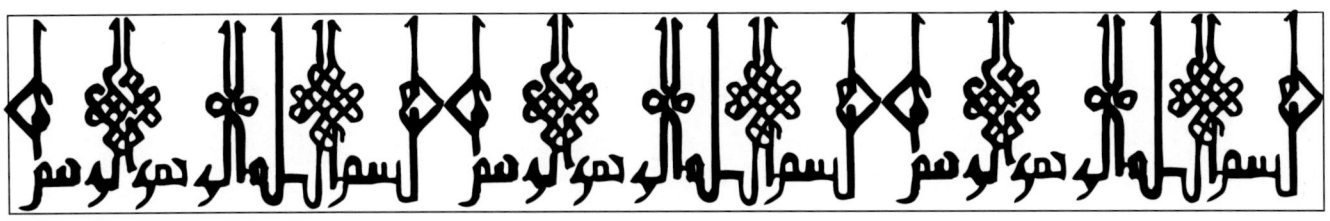

How Much do You Know about Muslims?

Research the following. Tick the answer that is correct.

1. Muslims live

   (a)   in Saudi Arabia. ☐

   (b)   mainly in the Middle East. ☐

   (c)   all over the world. ☐

2. The symbol of Islam is

   (a)   a full moon. ☐

   (b)   a cross. ☐

   (c)   a crescent moon and star. ☐

3. What happened in the year 622 CE, when the Muslim calendar begins?

   (a)   Muhammad went to Medina. ☐

   (b)   Muhammad met the angel. ☐

   (c)   Muhammad was born. ☐

4. It is a Muslim's duty to

   (a)   visit Mecca in their lifetime. ☐

   (b)   travel as much as possible. ☐

   (c)   stay at home. ☐

5. During the month of Ramadan, Muslims
   (a)   eat only during the hours of daylight. ☐

   (b)   eat only during the hours of darkness. ☐

   (c)   eat a ram. ☐

6. Muslims learn to read the Qur'an

   (a)   when they are an adult. ☐

   (b)   at secondary school. ☐

   (c)   when they are about five years old. ☐

7. Muslim women

   (a)   dress modestly. ☐

   (b)   all wear burkas. ☐

   (c)   all wear short skirts. ☐

8. Muslims should pray

   (a)   whenever they like. ☐

   (b)   five times a day. ☐

   (c)   at least once a week. ☐

9. Which two of these are Muslims not allowed?

   (a)   Fish. ☐

   (b)   Pork. ☐

   (c)   Eggs. ☐

   (d)   Alcohol. ☐

10. Which one of these countries does not have a population which is over 90% Muslim?

   (a)   Indonesia. ☐

   (b)   Somalia. ☐

   (c)   Brazil. ☐

   (d)   Pakistan. ☐

The Name of God

Muslims always begin their prayers with the words:
In the name of Allah, the compassionate, the merciful.
This is how the name of Allah is written in Arabic.

Muslims also use many other adjectives to describe Allah.

1. **Write ten adjectives that a Muslim might use to praise Allah.**

_____   _____

_____   _____

_____   _____

_____   _____

_____   _____

2. **Write something about your own faith, using a beautiful script. Decorate your work in an Islamic style.**

Complete the newspaper front page to retell the story of the Night of Power. Write the story and draw the mountain as if you were a journalist interviewing Muhammad and his family for a modern newspaper.

MECCA TIMES

Missing man returns

_____

_____

_____

_____

_____

_____

Amazing story from local father

_____

_____

_____

_____

_____

_____

Did he see an angel?

_____

_____

_____

_____

_____

_____

_____

_____

The mountain where local man
Muhammad claims he met an angel.

Now he can read

_____

_____

_____

_____

_____

_____

_____

_____

_____

_____

_____

_____

_____

_____

_____

_____

Teachers Notes

Religion: Sikhism

Curriculum Links:

R.E. Attainment Target 1: Learning about Religions
- Beliefs and teachings – describe religious beliefs and teachings and their importance.
- Expression and language – make links between religious symbols, language and stories and the beliefs or ideas that underlie them.

R.E. Attainment Target 2: Learning from Religion
- Identity and experience – compare aspects of their own experiences and those of others, identifying what influences their lives.
- Values and commitments – ask questions about matters of right and wrong and show understanding of moral and religious issues.

QCA R.E. Scheme of Work Reference
- 6A – Worship and community.

National Literacy Strategy Reference
- Year 6, Term 1, Text 14 – develop the skills of biographical writing in role.

Story Reference:

Stories from the Sikh World by Rani and Jugnu Singh (MacDonald, 1988).
Storyteller Series: Sikh Stories by Anita Ganeri (Evans, 2001).
Modern World Religions: Sikhism by John Mayled (Heinemann, 2002).
World Beliefs and Cultures: Sikhism by Sue Penny (Heinemann, 2000).
Keystones: Gurdwara (A&C Black, 1998).

Notes – Pages 77 and 78 – The Merchant and the Five Hundred Gold Coins:

Introduction:
- Read the story to the class. Stop at various points in the story and ask the children to predict what is going to happen next and why.

Discussion:
- Ask the class what they would have done if they had been Makham Shah when he thought his boat would sink.
- Having been saved, did Makham Shah have to fulfil his promise?
- Would anyone have known if he had not?
- Ask the children for their solutions to the puzzle he had to solve to find the true Guru.
- Why was it a good idea to give a couple of coins away?

Extension:
- Tegh Bahadur was the great uncle of Guru Har Krishan. How might knowing this have made finding the Guru easier?
- Discuss the 'passing on' of religious leadership. The story of Samuel finding the child David in the Bible could be read, the finding of the next Dalai Lama could be researched, or the choosing of Christian leaders: the Pope; the Patriarch or the Archbishop of Canterbury.

Notes – Page 79 – The Ten Gurus:

Introduction/Discussion:
- Explain about the founding of the Sikh religion by Guru Nanak. Explain that nine other Gurus followed him as head of the religion. Some of these were related to the Guru who went before; some were appointed or selected for the important task of leading the Sikh community as their Guru.
- Remind children that when completing research, they should read the articles and make their own notes, not just copy out the information.

Resources:
- Pencil or pen and crayons
- Non-fiction books about the Sikh Gurus
- ICT opportunity – use a computer with the Internet or CD–ROM encyclopaedia for research

Answers:

Name	Born	Became Guru	Died	Remembered for
Guru Nanak	1469	1520	1539	Set up the first Sikh community in Kartapur.
Guru Angad	1504	1539	1552	Collected the hymns of Guru Nanak, with some of his own hymns.
Guru Amar Das	1479	1552	1574	Encouraged the tradition of communal eating in the langar.
Guru Ram Das	1534	1574	1581	Founded the sacred city of Amritsar.
Guru Arjan	1563	1581	1606	The first Sikh martyr, he was tortured to death by the Mogul emperor.
Guru Hargobind	1595	1606	1644	The 'Warrior' Guru, he trained Sikhs to fight to defend themselves.
Guru Har Rai	1630	1644	1661	Set up free medicine for the sick.
Guru Har Krishan	1656	1661	1664	A child of five when he became Guru, he died at eight of smallpox.
Guru Tegh Bahadur	1621	1664	1675	His name means 'brave sword'. He fought the Mogul rulers and was executed.
Guru Gobind Singh	1666	1675	1708	He formed the Khalsa, the community of the Five Ks. He also chose the Adi Granth, the holy book of the Sikhs as the next Guru. It became known as Guru Granth Sahib.

Notes – Page 80 – Worship and Community:

Resources:
- Pencil or pen
- Non-fiction books about world religions
- ICT opportunity – use a computer with the Internet or CD-ROM encyclopaedia for research

Answers:

Teacher check, but could include:

Sikh values	Why important	Own life	Other religions
Take a bath before going to the Gurdwara.	Sign of respect, particularly to the 'Guru' Granth Sahib.	Bathe before party or special occasion.	Islam: wash before prayers.
Give offerings of food and money.	Ritual within Sikh worship – Sikh's view service to the community as very important.	Many schools participate in 'Red Nose Day', where the money raised is used to help others.	Christianity: Harvest festival and charities; e.g. Oxfam.
Men and women sit in separate groups during worship.	Often so men and women do not distract one another during the worship.	Not common in the western world, although we do have some single sex schools.	Judaism: in Orthodox churches, men and women pray separately. Islam: only men are allowed in the main prayer hall of the mosque.
During worship there are readings from the holy book.	The readings from the Guru Granth Sahib give worshippers a spiritual message.	School assemblies contain collective worship, often from the Bible or other religious text.	Christianity: the Bible. Judaism: the Torah. Islam: the Qur'an.
Songs of praise are sung during worship.	There are special songs of praise, played by trained musicians, which have meaning to Sikh worshippers.	We have several special songs – national anthems, football team songs; etc.	Christianity: hymns. Hinduism: mantras.
The Sikh community has a day of rest.	This is a day for families to gather and visit the Gurdwara.	Weekends give us a break from school and work.	Christianity: Sunday. Judaism: Saturday. Islam: Friday.
Family occasions are celebrated together.	Family is very important to Sikhs. Weddings and naming ceremonies are joyful occasions.	Celebrations of family occasions include weddings and milestone birthdays; e.g. 21st.	Most religions have special ceremonies for welcoming children into the religion, marriage and death.
Important anniversaries and festivals are celebrated.	Sikhs have two kinds of festivals: those which celebrate events in the lives of the Gurus and those which are held on the same day as Hindu festivals, but have special Sikh meaning; e.g. Holi, Diwali.	In Britain we have holidays at Christmas and Easter, plus other Bank holidays. Other countries also have special days; e.g. 4 July in the USA.	Christianity: Christmas and Easter. Judaism: Passover. Islam: Eid. Hinduism: Diwali. Buddhism: Festival of the Tooth.

Notes – Page 81 – Biography of a Guru:

Introduction/Discussion:
- What is a biography? Have any children ever read a biography? If so, who was it about and what do they remember about it? Show children examples of biographies.
- Recap the importance of research and keeping notes. Discuss how to research a person, the tools to use and what to look for. Make some suggestions about effective note taking.
- This task is also ideal for partner or small-group work.

Extension:
- When the biographies are written and illustrated, make a class display.

Resources:
- Pencil or pen and crayons
- Selection of biographies
- Non-fiction books about the Sikh Gurus
- ICT opportunity – use a computer with the Internet or CD-ROM encyclopaedia for research

Answers:
Teacher check

The Merchant and the Five Hundred Gold Coins

The eighth Sikh Guru, Har Krishan, told the Sikhs that the next Guru would be found in the small village of Bakala in north-west India, near Amritsar. He did not realise that this would cause chaos in Bakala. Almost immediately every man in Bakala was saying that he, and only he, was the true heir of Har Krishan. Everyone knew that the Sikh movement was prosperous, and the Guru would have access to great wealth. Many wealthy followers of the religion gave large donations to the Gurus to use in their work with the poor and needy. Of course, the true Guru would not use the money for his own ends, but many unscrupulous men thought they could have access to this great wealth. It was a wealthy merchant named Makham Shah who discovered the true identity of the next Sikh Guru.

Makham Shah was a wealthy merchant who traded in silks and exotic perfumes. One day, as he sailed along the west coast of India, a storm blew up. Makham had a large cargo on board and he was concerned that the storm seemed to come from nowhere. It was a ferocious storm. The sea became a cauldron and the rain and wind lashed his boat. The thunderclaps rent the sky and the lightning lit up the tiny boat. Makham had never seen anything like it in all his years sailing up and down the coast. The crew were bailing out water and trying to keep the boat from turning over or sailing onto the rocks. Everyone was wet and frightened, they were cold and night was coming on. Makham Shah was frightened for himself, his crew and his boat. He thought they would surely be lost.

The Merchant and the Five Hundred Gold Coins

He closed his eyes and began to pray. He said, 'Please, God, hear my prayer, save my life and those of my companions. Do not let my ship sink. I will give the Guru five hundred gold coins in thanks if we survive this storm'.

As he opened his eyes, he was amazed. The storm was receding, the sea was becoming calm, the rain had stopped and the black clouds were blowing out to sea. He could see land ahead, and they would be in safe harbour shortly. As he sailed into the harbour, he was relieved that they had all been saved and he thanked God.

He remembered his promise and the next day he set off for the village of Bakala to give his donation to the Guru. But when he arrived in Bakala he found he had a problem. Which was the true Guru, to whom he should give his 500 gold coins? There were hundreds of men, all claiming to be the one true Guru. After some thought, Makham Shah had an idea. He decided to visit each of those claiming to be the true Guru and to offer them two gold coins. He decided that the fake gurus would take the coins and only the true Guru would know how much he had promised to donate in his hour of need.

He set off to the first house where a man sat praying. Makham Shah bowed and placed two gold coins in his hand. The man thanked him, and told him that he had done well to come straight to the true Guru. But Makham Shah left knowing this was not the true Guru. He continued through the village. To each claimant he gave two gold coins. each thanked him and praised him for finding the true Guru, but none asked for the promised number of coins. By lunchtime Makham Shah was tired and dispirited. He didn't know if he could find the true Guru. He asked an old man walking along the street if he know of any other gurus. The old man told him about Tegh Bahadur, a quiet man who prayed a lot and lived outside the village.

Makham Shah set off again in the direction the old man had said. Just beyond the village there was a small simple hut. Inside, a man prayed quietly. Makham Shah bowed and placed two gold coins in his hand. Tegh Bahadur looked at him and then looked at the coins. 'Have you forgotten your promise?' he asked. 'When your life and that of your crew was in danger you promised five hundred gold coins, not two. Isn't that right?'

Makham Shah was humble and overjoyed. He gave the whole five hundred gold coins to Tegh Bahadur and gave thanks. Then he rushed back to the village, to tell everyone that he had found the one true Guru. 'Tegh Bahadur is the one true Guru,' he shouted.

The Ten Gurus

The first Sikh Guru was Guru Nanak. Nine Gurus followed him. The last Guru, Guru Gobind Singh, said that after him there would be no more human Gurus. Instead, all of the knowledge and guidance Sikhs needed would be found in the holy book of scriptures, Guru Granth Sahib.

Research the ten Sikh Gurus to complete this table.

Name	Born	Became Guru	Died	Remembered for
Guru Nanak	1469	1520	1539	
Guru Angad	1504	1539	1552	
Guru Amar Das	1479	1552	1574	
Guru Ram Das	1534	1574	1581	
Guru Arjan	1563	1581	1606	
Guru Hargobind	1595	1606	1644	
Guru Har Rai	1630	1644	1661	
Guru Har Krishan	1656	1661	1664	
Guru Tegh Bahadur	1621	1664	1675	
Guru Gobind Singh	1666	1675	1708	

Worship and Community

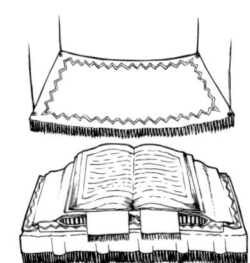

*Worship and community are very important to Sikhs.
Through worship they express their faith and talk to God,
both as a community and individually.*

1. **Read the important values of the worship and community of Sikhs.**

2. **Research and write why these values are important to Sikhs, similar aspects of your own life and similar aspects of other religions.**

Sikh values	Why the values are important to Sikhs	Similar aspects of my own life	Similar aspects of other religions
Take a bath before going to the Gurdwara.			
Give offerings of food and money.			
Men and women sit in separate groups during worship.			
During worship there are readings from the holy book.			
Songs of praise are sung during worship.			
The Sikh community has a day of rest.			
Family occasions are celebrated together.			
Important anniversaries and festivals are celebrated.			

Biography of a Guru

1. **Choose one of the ten Sikh Gurus. Research his life and make notes below.**

    (a) The Guru I have chosen is _____

    (b) Personal data _____

    _____

    _____

    _____

    (c) Important incidents

    • _____

    • _____

    • _____

    • _____

    • _____

    • _____

    (d) Key achievements

    • _____

    • _____

    • _____

    • _____

    (e) Resources used _____

    _____

    _____

    _____

2. **Use your notes to write the biography of your chosen Sikh Guru.**

Teachers Notes

Religion: Buddhism

Curriculum Links:

R.E. Attainment Target 1: Learning about Religions

- Beliefs and teachings – describe religious beliefs and teachings and their importance.

R.E. Attainment Target 2: Learning from Religion

- Meaning and purpose – compare their own and other people's ideas about questions that are difficult to answer.
- Values and commitments – ask questions about matters of right and wrong and show understanding of moral and religious issues.

QCA R.E. Scheme of Work Reference

- 6C – Why are sacred texts important?

National Literacy Strategy Reference

- Year 6, Term 1, Text 9 – prepare a short section of a story as a script.

Story Reference:

Storyteller Series: Buddhist Stories by Anita Ganeri (Evans Brothers, 2001).
Religious Education Topics (Longman, 1989).
Discovering Sacred Texts: Buddhist Scriptures Owen Cole (Editor) (Heinemann, 1994).
Keystones: Buddhist Vihara by Anita Ganeri (A&C Black, 1998).
World Beliefs and Cultures: Buddhism by Sue Penny (Heinemann, 2000).

Notes – Pages 85 and 86 – Kisa Gotami:

Introduction:

- Before embarking on this unit of work, ascertain if any children have recently had a death in their family. Be sensitive to their emotions at this time.
- Buddha wanted people to understand that death is a part of everyone's experience. This reflects a Buddhist belief in the impermanence of life.
- Tell the children that Buddha's teachings were all oral (he left no written body of thought), often using stories. These 'stories' or 'parables' were to help followers see the lessons for themselves.
- The Dhammapada contains much of the Buddha's teaching, but it is not considered an authoritative scripture like in other religions.
- Ask children to name some parables or teachings from the Bible, or other religious books you have been studying.

Discussion:

- Why did Kisa Gotami believe her son was ill?
- What did she want from Buddha?
- Why didn't Buddha tell her that her son was dead?
- Why did Buddha send her around the village?
- Why did Buddha teach about death in this way?
- Discuss childrens' reactions to the story and to the underlying theme of death.

Extension:

- Buddhists believe in life after death (Nirvana). Research biblical references to life after death (1 Corinthians, Chapter 15, Verse 20) Muslims also have a description of paradise; it is a garden described in the Qur'an (Surahs 55 and 76).
- Research other 'parables' from the Dhammapada, or from the Bible. Look for common themes.

Notes – Page 87 – Buddha's Teachings:

Introduction/Discussion:

- The eight-fold path consists of: right understanding; right thinking; right speech; right action; right livelihood; right effort; right-mindfulness; and right contemplation.
- The Five Precepts (or promises): Not to harm any other being; Not to take anything which is not given; Not to misuse their senses; Not to harm others with their words; Not to take drugs or other substances which cloud the mind.

Resources:

- Pencil or pen
- Story of Kisa Gotami

Answers:

1. Kisa Gotami's son had died, but she thought that he was just ill and that medicine would bring him back to life.
2. (a) Mustard seeds from a house in which no-one has died.
   (b) Buddha knew this would be impossible to find.
3. Kisa Gotami
4. Kisa Gotami realised that in every family someone had died and that this was natural and unchangeable.
5. Teacher check
6. Teacher check, but possible answers include:

Teaching:	Where found:
Do what God (your religion) asks.	Torah and Bible: Genesis, Chapter 22.
Help others who have been hurt.	Bible: Luke, Chapter 10, Verse 30.
Rules from God.	Torah and Bible.
Qur'an was revealed to prophet Muhammad.	Qur'an: Surah 96.
The Mool Mantar.	Guru Granth Sahib.

Notes – Page 88 – Guidelines for Living:

Introduction/Discussion:

- Discuss each of the precepts as a whole class.
- With each precept, encourage children to think from minor infringements to major ones.
- Encourage children to think of the precepts from a different point of view; e.g. how might a vegetarian interpret the first precept?
- Change the context of the Five Precepts – think about home and school.

Extension:

- Extend the comparison between the Five Precepts and the Ten Commandments to other religions; e.g. the Five Pillars of Islam.
- In groups, children could develop scenarios related to the Five Precepts and write and perform them for the rest of the class.

Resources:

- Pencil or pen and crayons
- Bibles

Answers:

1. Teacher check, but could include:
   (a) Hitting siblings/peers; hitting someone during a game; throwing stones at an animal.
   (b) Shoplifting; stealing from siblings/peers.
   (c) Eating more than they need.
   (d) Bullying; unkindness to siblings/parents/peers.
   (e) Smoking; drinking alcohol; taking illegal drugs.

2.

Precept	Commandment
Do not harm others with words.	Honour thy father and thy mother.
Do not harm any other living thing.	Thou shalt not kill.
Do not take anything that is not given.	Thou shalt not steal.

Notes – Page 89 – Kisa Gotami's Son:

Introduction/Discussion:

- Retell the story using improvisation.
- Look at plays, examine how they differ from stories.
- List the differences in organisation: no speech marks, no use of words like 'said', each person's speech presented separately, inclusion of stage directions.
- Discuss setting, props and character descriptions.

Extension:

- In groups, perform their script, ensuring that each group member has a role-acting or directing.

Resources:

- Pencil or pen
- Selection of plays
- Story of Kisa Gotami

Kisa Gotami and her Dead Son

This story tells us how Buddha taught by giving people a task to perform, so that they learned the lesson for themselves.

During Buddha's time there lived a woman called Kisa Gotami. She had a son. She looked after her son with great love and care. However, the child died as soon as he was able to walk. Kisa Gotami was grief stricken.

It is Buddhist practice to cremate a dead body. Kisa Gotami, who had not seen death before, did not allow the body of her beloved son to be cremated. She thought that her son was ill and wanted to find some medicine to bring him back to life.

Kisa Gotami went from house to house, carrying the body of her dead son. At every house, Kisa Gotami asked, 'Have you got any medicine to cure my son?'

The people replied, 'That boy is dead. No medicine will bring him back to life'.

Finally, Kisa Gotami came to the house of a wise man. The man felt that he should help Kisa Gotami, and said 'I do not know of any such medicine, but go and ask Gotama Buddha. He will tell you of a suitable medicine'.

So Kisa Gotami went to the Buddha and asked him if he knew of any medicine that would cure her son.

'Yes,' said the Buddha. 'I know of a medicine for this purpose. Go and get some mustard seeds from a house in which no one has died.'

Kisa Gotami thanked the Buddha. Carrying the body of her dead son, she went in search of the mustard seeds.

At each house, she said, 'The Buddha has asked me to bring him some mustard seeds from a house in which no one has died, as medicine for my dead son. Is this such a house?'

The householders replied, 'We are very sorry, but one of our family died in this house some time ago'.

This was the reply Kisa Gotami received at every house in the town. Therefore, she did not get any mustard seeds.

Kisa Gotami realised that in every house and in every family, someone had died. She realised that in the whole town, the number of people who had died was more than those who were living.

Kisa Gotami went to Buddha and said, 'It is impossible to get the mustard seeds that you asked me to get. Someone has died in every house and in every family'.

Kisa Gotami and her Dead Son

The Buddha explained that his medicine was really for Kisa Gotami, and not for her son. 'You imagined that only your son was dead, but this is the constant lot of being.'

Buddha explained the Dhamma to her and spoke this verse:

> *Death seizes and carries away*
>
> *The worldly man, whose mind*
>
> *Is set on families and on owning herds of cattle,*
>
> *As a great flood carries away a sleeping village.*
>
> *(The Dhammapada, Verse 287)*

The Buddha granted Kisa Gotami's request to be admitted into the order of nuns. Later, on a day when it was her turn to light the lamp in the meeting hall, she observed the flame. Kisa Gotami noticed the movement and continuity of the flame and remarked:

> *Even so it is with living creatures,*
> *they rise and pass away, and on attaining Nirvana they are no*
> *more known.*

The Buddha understood Kisa Gotami's thoughts and said:

> *Rather than live a hundred years,*
>
> *But not achieve Nirvana,*
>
> *Better is the life of a single day*
>
> *For him who sees Nirvana.*

Buddha's Teachings

1. Why did Kisa Gotami ask for the Buddha's help? _____

   _____

2. (a) What medicine did the Buddha suggest to Kisa Gotami? _____

   _____

   (b) Why? _____

   _____

3. Who was the medicine supposed to help? _____

4. How did the medicine actually help? _____

5. Tick the lesson you think the Buddha wanted Kisa Gotami to learn.

   (a) ☐ You can't bring someone back to life.

   (b) ☐ Everyone has had unhappiness in their life.

   (c) ☐ Mustard seeds help the bereaved. (d) ☐ We must accept our fate.

   (e) ☐ Suffering helps us to learn. (f) ☐ Nothing is permanent.

There are many lessons contained in the teachings of the Buddha.

There are also lessons in the teachings of Jesus and other prophets.

6. Research two important teachings in your community and list where these teachings come from. They may come from more than one religion or prophet.

Teaching	Where found

Guidelines for Living

The Buddhist scriptures are important because they contain guidelines for living. The scriptures help Buddhists live a life of compassion and respect for themselves and for other people. The Five Precepts are essential guidelines for all Buddhists. They tell Buddhists that they should not:

- **Harm any other being.**
- **Take anything which is not given.**
- **Misuse their senses.**
- **Harm others with their words.**
- **Take drugs or other substances which cloud the mind.**

1. **Beside each Precept, draw a picture of something that would not be acceptable to Buddhists. Write why.**

	Precept	Something which would not be acceptable to Buddhists	Why
(a)	Do not harm any other being.		
(b)	Do not take anything which is not given.		
(c)	Do not misuse their senses.		
(d)	Do not harm others with their words.		
(e)	Do not take drugs or other substances which cloud the mind.		

2. **The Christian religion has Ten Commandments. Find these in the Bible. Discuss how they are similar to the Five Precepts of the Buddhist religion.**

Kisa Gotami's Son

Write notes to help you to write a script of the Kisa Gotami story. Include a setting and character descriptions. Stage directions will need to be included throughout your play. Once your notes are complete, use them to write a full script of the Kisa Gotami story.

Setting: _____

Character Descriptions:

Kisa Gotami _____

Buddha _____

Wise Man _____

Villager 1 _____

Villager 2 _____

Villager 3 _____

Stage directions: _____

Kisa Gotami: _____

Villager 1: _____

Stage directions: _____

Kisa Gotami: _____

Wise Man: _____

Stage directions: _____

Kisa Gotami: _____

Buddha: _____

Stage directions: _____

Kisa Gotami: _____

Villager 2: _____

Kisa Gotami: _____

Villager 3: _____

Stage directions: _____

Kisa Gotami: _____

Buddha: _____

Kisa Gotami: _____